MEL BAY PRESENTS

UNDERSTANDING HOW TO BUILD GUITAR CHORDS & ARPEGGIOS

BY
MICHAEL
POLICASTRO

Visit us on the Web at http://www.melbay.com — E-mail us at email@melbay.com

Contents

I. Theory

II. The Guitar

Preface

Most people who have studied the guitar are familiar with the assortment of "One Million and One Guitar Chords" type books available today. Though these books contain an abundance of chords, they leave many beginning to intermediate guitar students overwhelmed and puzzled, failing to yield any real understanding of where chords come from or how to build them. In addition, using this sort of book a student may find a particular chord by name, yet may poorly apply the chord shown in the diagram having no idea how to manipulate, voice or apply this chord to fulfill his musical vision in a particular situation. This type of book seems to, as the saying goes, give guitar students a "fish to eat for a day" rather than *teaching them how* to "fish to eat for a lifetime."

Consequently, the first part of *"Understanding How to Build Guitar Chords and Arpeggios"* teaches a very specific portion of music theory with the goal of providing thoroughly the necessary foundation for building chords and arpeggios. The second part reveals the unique fingerboard patterns arising from the nature of the guitar's six string tuning, and applies these essential patterns teaching every aspect of building chords and arpeggios *for the guitar*. Clear illustrations are abundant throughout this text making this wealth of information much easier to learn and apply. Similarly, this book is accessible to those who never learned to read music notation, and even those who never want to, presenting ideas everyone can understand and utilize. Moreover, self-tests are at the end of each chapter facilitating complete and thorough learning.

While *"Understanding How to Build Guitar Chords and Arpeggios"* is a comprehensive and thorough study, this text omits the enormous subject of harmonic (chord) progression as this requires in-depth study all it's own. Study of harmonic progression, however, *is necessary* for those seeking a complete education in music. Undoubtedly, this book will help make sense out of other types of chord books already in one's possession, and prove an invaluable treasure to those studying melodic improvisation, too.

Though this text accelerates rapidly through intermediate and advanced levels, and may take a lifetime to master, even the beginner with no musical experience will find the subject matter logically revealed and readily accessible. Don't be discouraged, however, when finding the need to review certain subjects repeatedly, as this material requires much repetitious study. Patience and persistence pay large dividends!

For those who have no experience with the guitar, or music in general, first refer to Appendixes 1 and 2 to help understand the diagrams in this book and to learn to tune the guitar. Ultimately, for anyone wanting to master the guitar, we recommend finding a qualified and experienced guitar instructor who can give proper guidance and answer any questions.

Acknowledgements and Dedication

Special thanks to my guitar students whose eagerness to learn and appreciated prompting helped provide the catalyst for this book, especially Phil Aklonis and Janice Grant who gave unselfishly of their time and friendship. Thanks also to Jeff Becker, a fellow professional and brother for his time, talent, experience and charitable criticism; and to Jim Hovey at *Victor's House of Music* for being more than gracious in providing a way to make this book available.

Very special thanks to my wife Yvette whose faithful love, constant encouragement, and personal sacrifice not only helped make this book possible, but continually fills my life with much joy, peace and love.

Most of all, thanks to God "from whom every good endowment and perfect gift comes".

This book is lovingly dedicated to my parents: for years of guitar lessons, decades of patience, and a lifetime of love and parenting.

CHAPTER 1
THE MUSICAL ALPHABET

Music has its own alphabet representing specific pitches, or tones. This alphabet repeats itself every twelve tones, or every twelfth fret along any single guitar string (each fret representing one tone). For example, the fifth guitar string is tuned to the tone named "A". The name of the tone at the twelfth fret of the fifth string is also "A". The musical alphabet has twelve members beginning with the letter-name "A", repeating itself in cyclical fashion every twelve tones. Musical tones may infinitely increase or decrease in pitch, yet the finite musical alphabet always repeats itself every twelve tones.

Figure 1-1

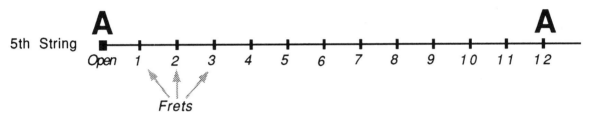

More accurately, the distance from one fret to the next closest fret (in either direction) is called a half-tone, or half-step. In the above example, twelve half-tones are actually counted from letter-name "A", the beginning of the musical alphabet, to letter-name "A", the beginning of another cycle of the musical alphabet.

Figure 1-2

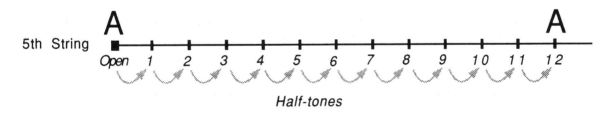

In addition, two half-tones equal one whole-tone, or whole-step. Therefore, there are six whole-tones from "A" to "A".

Figure 1-3

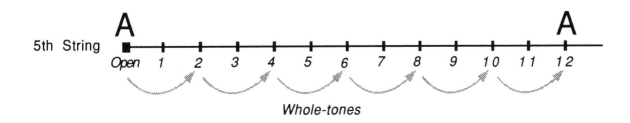

Figure 1-4 shows some other members of the musical alphabet.

Figure 1-4

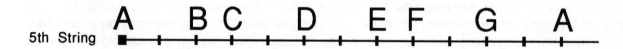

Though these other alphabet members seem predictable enough, notice how they vary in distance from one to the other. All letter-names of the musical alphabet are separated by a whole-tone except for "B" and "C", and "E" and "F", which are separated by half-tones, as illustrated in Figure 1-5.

Figure 1-5

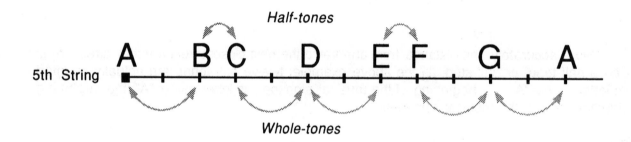

The names of the alphabet members between these basic letter-names are all that remain. First, learn these simple terms and their symbols:

1. Sharp (♯) – Make this tone higher in pitch by a half-step —or—
    this tone is a half-step higher in pitch than its letter-name;

2. Flat (♭) -- Make this tone lower in pitch by a half-step —or—
    this tone is a half-step lower in pitch than its letter-name;

3. Natural (♮) -- Cancel a previous sharp or flat —or—
    this tone is neither sharp nor flat.

To find the remaining members of the musical alphabet begin with the tone named "D" at the fifth fret of the fifth string (A), for example. The tone a half-step higher in pitch than "D" is called "D sharp" (written D♯). The tone a half-step lower in pitch than "D" is called "D flat" (written D♭). Or, in other words, the tone located at the sixth fret of the fifth string is called "D♯" because it is a half-step higher in pitch than "D"; likewise, the tone located at the fourth fret of the fifth string is called " D♭" because it is a half-step lower in pitch than "D".

Figure 1-6

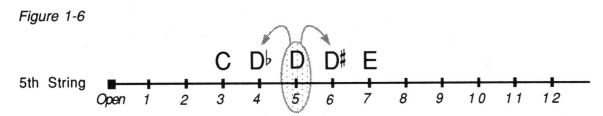

But what about "C♯" or "E♭"? Notice that the tone located at the fourth fret of the fifth string is also a half-step higher in pitch than "C" as well as a half-step lower in pitch than "D". Likewise, the tone located at the sixth fret of the fifth string is a half-step lower in pitch than "E" as well as a half-step higher in pitch than "D". Therefore, these two tones may also be called "C♯" and "E♭", respectively.

Figure 1-7

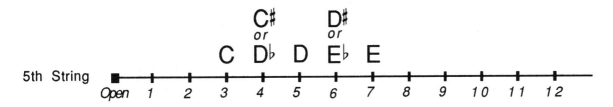

In musical terms, two letter-names naming the same tone are called *enharmonic*. In other words, "C♯" is enharmonic with "D♭" because they name the same tone; this is also true of "E♭" and "D♯".

Figure 1-8 shows the entire musical alphabet. Notice the enharmonic equivalents of "C♭" and "B", "B♯" and "C", "F♭" and "E", "E♯" and "F". Be familiar with these as well.

Figure 1-8

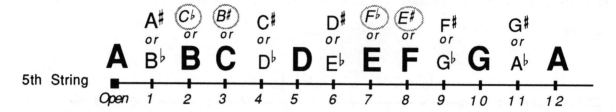

Taking this illustration a step further, look at the musical alphabet shown in Figure 1-9 as the "circle of half-tones".

Figure 1-9

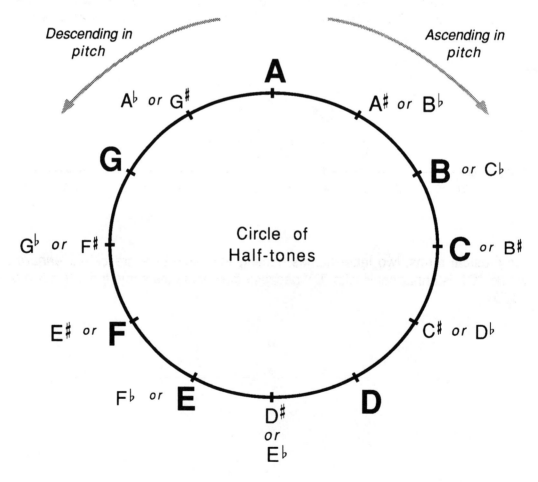

Figure 1-9 perhaps presents the musical alphabet more clearly in cyclical form. Whether beginning at "A" or any other member of the musical alphabet, one will arrive at the same letter-name again after moving twelve half-tones in either direction.

It is, therefore, possible to play several different tones on the guitar with the same letter-name as illustrated in Figure 1-10. Play these tones in Figure 1-10 on the guitar. They all have the same letter-name (E), yet they are different pitches.

Figure 1-10

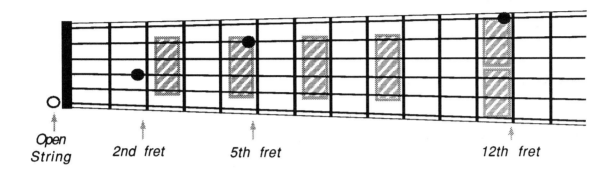

Open
String   2nd fret   5th fret   12th fret

If you are given the name of any guitar string, do you think you could figure out the names of all the tones on that string? (Refer to Appendix 1 to find the names of all six guitar strings.)

Let's figure out all the tones on the third string for example. Referring to the musical alphabet, or circle of half-tones, in Figure 1-9, begin at "G" in the diagram, and at the open third string of your guitar (the open third guitar string is named "G"). Begin ascending one fret, or one half-tone, at a time on your guitar while ascending one half-tone at a time on the diagram. So, the tone at the first fret of the third string is "G#" or "A♭", the tone at the second fret of the third string is an "A", the tone at the third fret of the third string is "A#" or "B♭", etc.

In this way the student may begin to figure out every tone on the guitar, or find any tone he desires.

TEST YOURSELF
CHAPTER 1

1. What is the distance from one fret to the next closest fret called?

   _____

2. Two half-tones equal(s) _____ whole tone(s).

3. The distance from "D" to "E" is a _____.

4. The distance from "E" to "F" is a _____.

5. Name the tone twelve half-steps higher than "F#".

   _____

6. Name the tone twelve half-steps lower than "A♭".

   _____

7. "This tone is a half-step higher in pitch than its letter-name" defines what musical term?

   _____

8. _____ is enharmonic with "G♭"; and

   "A#" is enharmonic with _____.

9. Name the tones on the sixth guitar string beginning with the open strings' name.

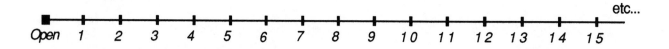

Open 1   2   3   4   5   6   7   8   9   10 11 12 13 14 15   etc...

10.   Name the tones in this fingerboard diagram.

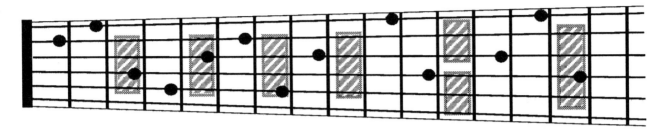

ANSWERS
TEST YOURSELF
CHAPTER 1

1. Half-step or half-tone

2. One

3. Whole-step or whole-tone

4. Half-step or half-tone

5. F♯

6. A♭

7. Sharp (♯)

8. F♯, B♭

9.

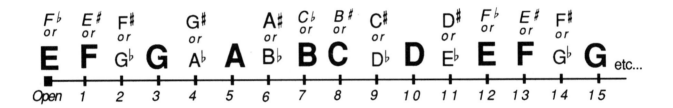

10.

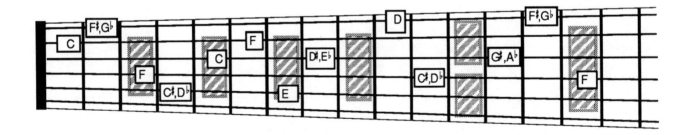

CHAPTER 2
THE MAJOR SCALE AND INTERVALS

A basic understanding of the major scale and intervals is an essential prerequisite to understanding arpeggios and chords. Guitar students especially, seem to leave intervals behind in theory books, neither understanding the benefits of their application nor learning to implement them in musical performance. To have a solid foundation for understanding arpeggios and chords, take the time to thoroughly study and comprehend this chapter.

A major scale is a series of eight tones, called scale degrees, adhering to a fixed (unchanging) pattern of half and whole steps from one tone to the next as depicted in Figure 2-1.

Figure 2-1

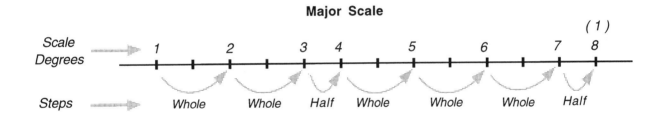

The eighth tone has the same letter name as the first tone, or tonic, and may also be considered another first tone itself as it begins another major scale. This fixed pattern of half and whole steps may be applied to the musical alphabet to produce all twelve possible major scales.

Let's try spelling a C Major scale. In other words, applying this fixed pattern of half and whole steps to the musical alphabet beginning with "C", we will determine the letter-names of the tones that make up the C major scale.

Figure 2-2

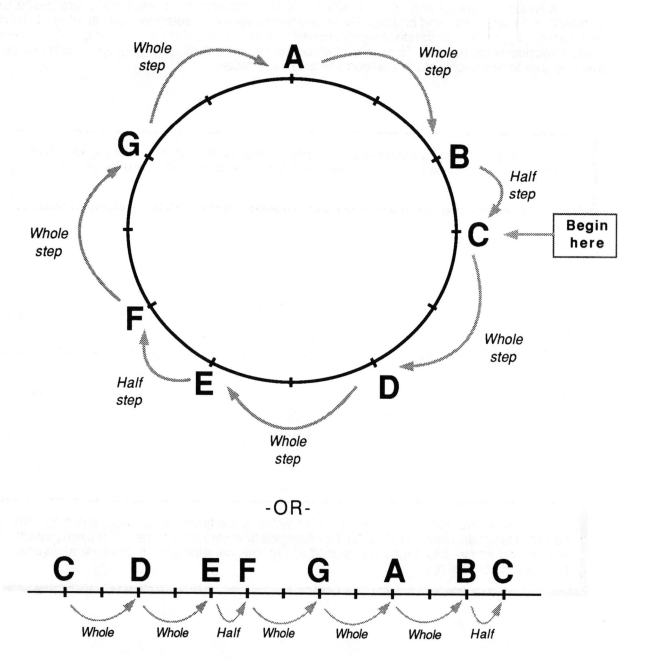

Notice the resulting letter-names are all "natural"; that is, there are no sharp or flat letter-names occurring in the C major scale.

Now, let's try spelling a G major scale. Applying this fixed pattern of half and whole steps to the musical alphabet beginning with "G", the following tones result shown in Figure 2-3.

Figure 2-3

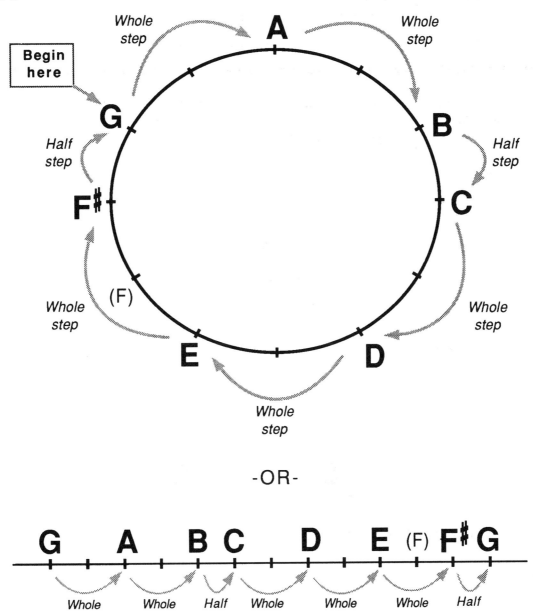

-OR-

Notice an "F♯" occurs in this scale. This tone is not called "G♭" because in this type of scale (major scale) **EACH LETTER-NAME IS USED ONLY ONCE.** (The spelling of all twelve major scales is found on page 24.)

Intervals

An interval is simply the relative position, or distance, of two tones, one to another. This distance is labeled two ways:
1) by numerical scale degrees with the beginning scale tone counted as 1 (one); and,
2) by qualitative names describing the type of interval. [1]

To begin, the following examples define a few intervals in simplest terms based only upon scale degrees. The interval from "C" ascending to "D" is called a "second" (2nd) because "D" is the second scale degree from the tonic "C".

Figure 2-4

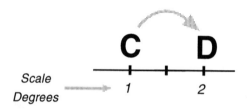

"C" ascending to "E" is an interval of a "third" (3rd).

Figure 2-5

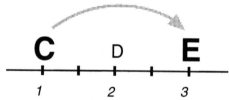

"C" ascending to "F" is an interval of a "fourth" (4th).

Figure 2-6

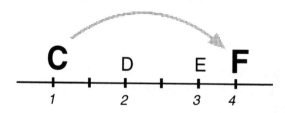

---

[1]   This is what differentiates intervals from half and whole tones. Half and whole tones represent a distance of sonic frequency determined by the equal tempered tuning method which divides an octave into twelve equal parts, or half tones.

"C" ascending to "C" is an interval of an "eighth", or an "octave" as it is commonly called.

Figure 2-7

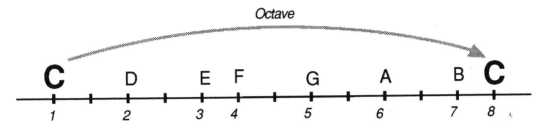

Octave

C   D   E F   G   A   B C
1   2   3 4   5   6   7 8

> Specifically, there are two basic types of intervals: *major* and *perfect*. Seconds (2nds), thirds (3rds), sixths (6ths), and sevenths (7ths) originate as *major*. Fourths (4ths), fifths (5ths) and octaves (and unisons, or primes, *See Unison Patterns, page 45*) originate as *perfect*.

With this new information, let's clarify our previous examples. From C ascending to D in Figure 2-4 is actually a *major* 2nd, from C ascending to E in Figure 2-5 is a *major* 3rd, from C ascending to F in Figure 2-6 is a *perfect* 4th, and from C ascending to C in Figure 2-7 is a *perfect* octave.

> There are three other types of intervals: *minor, augmented* and *diminished*.

> A minor interval is a half-tone lower than a major interval.

For example, from "C" ascending to "D♭" is a minor 2nd.

Figure 2-8

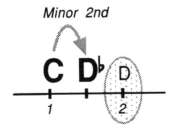

Minor 2nd

C D♭ D
1   2

From "C" ascending to "E♭" is a minor 3rd.

Figure 2-9

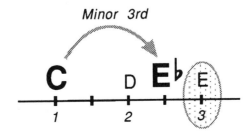

Minor 3rd

C   D E♭ E
1   2   3

From "C" ascending to "A♭" is a minor 6th.

Figure 2-10

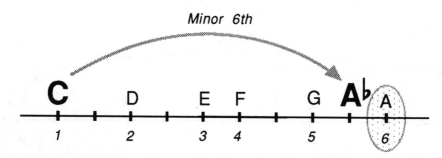

Next, | an augmented interval is a half-tone higher than a perfect or major interval. |

For example, from "C" ascending to "G♯" is an augmented 5th.

Figure 2-11

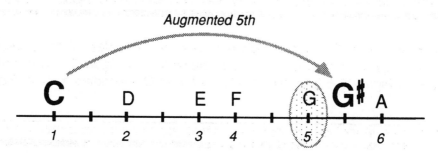

From "C" ascending to "D♯" is an augmented 2nd.

Figure 2-12

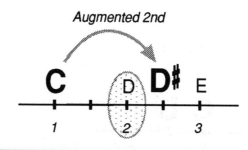

Before going any further, the definition of an interval needs to take on another facet, namely:

AN INTERVAL IS ALWAYS NUMBERED IN REFERENCE TO ITS LETTER-NAME.

Take another look at the previous examples. In Figure 2-10 the interval from "C" to "A♭" is a minor 6th, while in Figure 2-11 the interval from "C" to "G♯", the enharmonic equivalent of "A♭", is an augmented 5th. Likewise, in Figure 2-9, the interval from "C" to "E♭" is a minor 3rd, while in Figure 2-12 the interval from "C" to "D♯", the enharmonic equivalent of "E♭", is an augmented 2nd. Notice the link between a tone's letter-name and its consequent intervallic number. As in these previous examples, any letter-name of "A" has an intervallic number of a 6th; any letter-name of "G" has an intervallic number of a 5th, and any letter-name of "D" has an intervallic number of a 2nd, any letter-name of "E" has an intervallic number of a 3rd, regardless of whether they are major, minor, augmented, diminished, or perfect.

To continue, a diminished interval is a half-tone lower than a perfect or minor interval. For example, from "C" to "G♭" is a diminished 5th (Figure 2-13). Of special interest are the three whole-tones that make up the diminished 5th interval, dividing the octave exactly in half (an octave consists of six whole-tones). Consequently, the diminished 5th acquires a special name: Tritone.

Figure 2-13

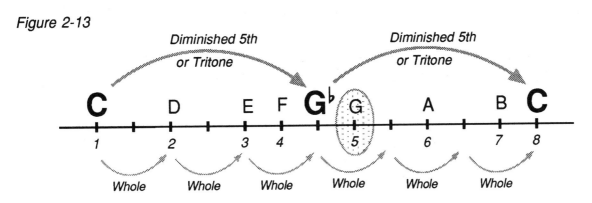

Because an interval is always numbered in reference to its letter-name, learning two more simple terms and their symbols is necessary before this next example.

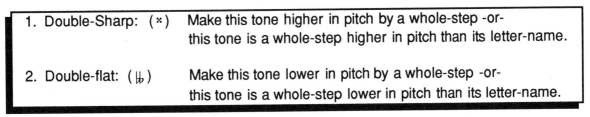

1. Double-Sharp: (ⅹ)   Make this tone higher in pitch by a whole-step -or-
                         this tone is a whole-step higher in pitch than its letter-name.

2. Double-flat: (♭♭)   Make this tone lower in pitch by a whole-step -or-
                         this tone is a whole-step lower in pitch than its letter-name.

Figure 2-14 shows the interval from "C" to "B♭♭" is a diminished 7th.

Figure 2-14

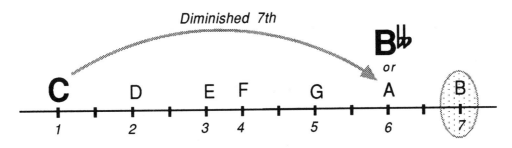

First, notice "B♭♭" is enharmonic with "A". Second, notice this interval is numbered a 7th, not a 6th because letter-name "B" is used, upholding our definition regarding the correlation between a tone's letter-name and its intervallic number. Consequently, this tone is named a diminished 7th interval (a minor 7th interval lowered by a half-tone), not a major 6th interval.

Intervals larger than an octave, called *compound intervals*, are numbered by continuing the numerical sequence into the next octave or more.

Figure 2-15

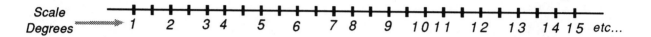

Notice in Figure 2-16 that the letter-name of the 9th through 15th scale degrees are identical to the 2nd through 8th (using the C major scale for example).

Figure 2-16

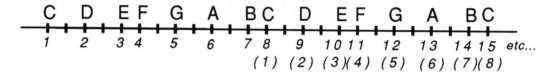

Consequently, the 9th, 10th, 13th and 14th intervals originate as major, and the 11th, 12th and 15th intervals originate as perfect. Likewise, all previously learned principles regarding intervals apply. For example,

From C ascending to the tone an octave higher than the nearest D is a major 9th.

Figure 2-17

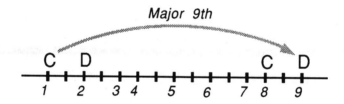

From C ascending to the tone an octave higher than the nearest A is a major 13th, etc.

Figure 2-18

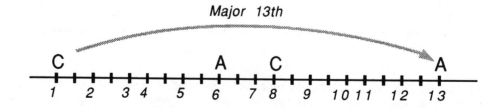

For more practice before concluding this chapter, let's look at some intervals using letter-names other than C as the beginning tone. Referring to the major scales on page 24 may help comprehension of the following examples.

From F ascending to A is a major 3rd.

Figure 2-19

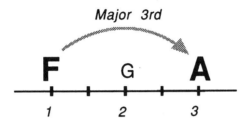

From G ascending to E♭ is a minor 6th.

Figure 2-20

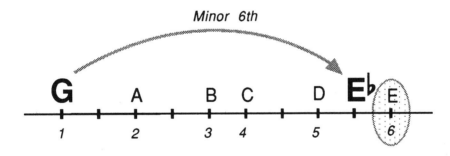

From D ascending to A is a perfect 5th.

Figure 2-21

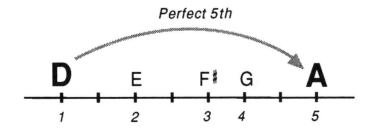

From B♭ ascending to F♭ is a diminished 5th.

Figure 2-22

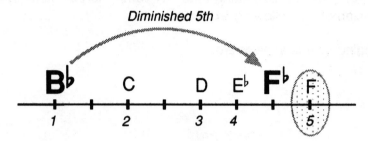

From E♭ ascending to B is an augmented 5th.

Figure 2-23

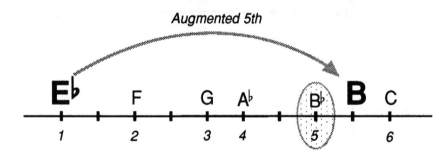

From A ascending to G♯ is a major 7th.

Figure 2-24

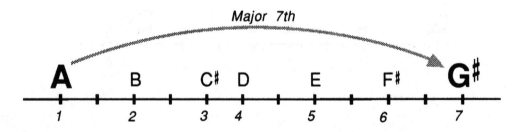

From A♭ ascending to B♭♭ is a minor 2nd. (A♭ ascending to A is an augmented prime.)

Figure 2-25

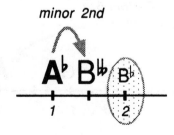

From D♭ ascending to the tone an octave higher than B♭ is a major 13th.

Figure 2-26

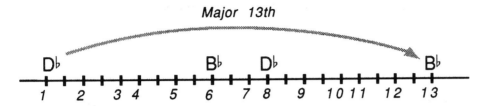

Major 13th

From G♭ ascending to C♭ is a perfect 4th. (From G♭ ascending to B is an augmented 3rd.)

Figure 2-27

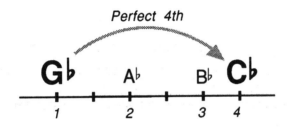

Perfect 4th

From C♭ ascending to G♭♭ is a diminished 5th. (From C♭ ascending to F is an augmented 4th.)

Figure 2-28

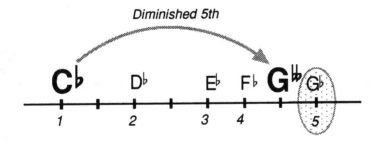

Diminished 5th

Interval Inversions

   In simplest terms, when an interval is *inverted* the lower tone becomes the higher tone or vice versa, that is, the order of the two tones is actually reversed.

Figure 2-29

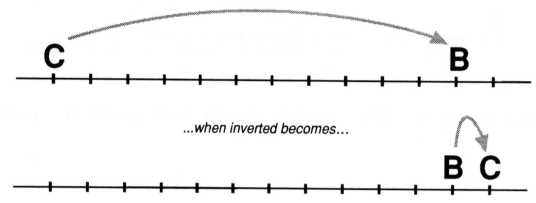

...when inverted becomes...

   The practical advantage to understanding how intervals invert is realizing there are *short cuts* to arriving at a particular tone. Knowing these short cuts helps a great deal when assembling various tones to build chords and arpeggios!

   To illustrate, "C" ascending to "B" is a major 7th, yet "B" ascending to "C" is a minor 2nd.

Figure 2-30

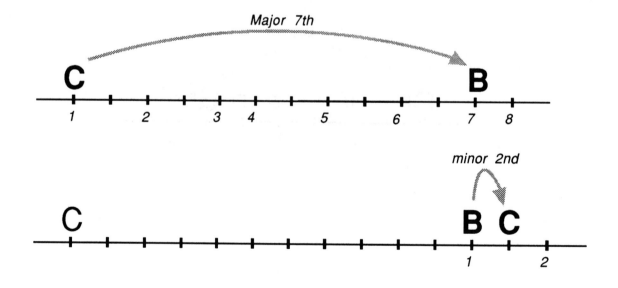

More to the point, instead of arriving at "B" by traveling the long distance of a an ascending major 7th, we can arrive at the same tone by the short distance of a *descending* minor 2nd.

Figure 2-31

Intervallic distances are the same whether ascending or descending. To avoid confusion therefore, simply learn to name and number intervals as *ascending*. Finding descending intervals is a slight change in perspective only, without the need for any mental "gymnastics".

The naming and numbering of interval inversions is entirely predictable, as summarized in Figure 2-32. Notice two things in particular: 1) the sum of each interval and its inversion equals an octave; and 2) both the descriptive name and number comprising an interval's name each have a corresponding inversion (e.g. a *Major* [name] *7th* [number] inverts to a *minor* [name] *2nd* [number]).

Figure 2-32

	Type of Interval	When Inverted Becomes
Names	Perfect	Perfect
	Major	minor
	minor	Major
	Augmented	diminished
	diminished	Augmented
Numbers	Unison (Prime)	Octave (8th)
	2nd	7th
	3rd	6th
	4th	5th
	5th	4th
	6th	3rd
	7th	2nd
	Octave (8th)	Unison (Prime)

Here are a few more examples:

Figure 2-33

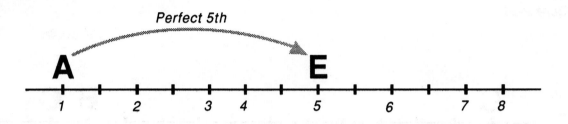

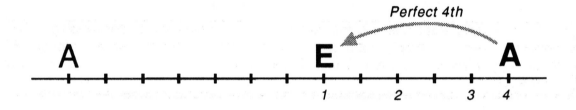

Figure 2-34

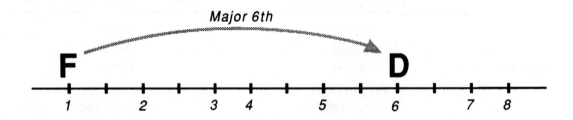

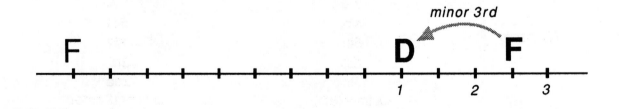

Figure 2-35

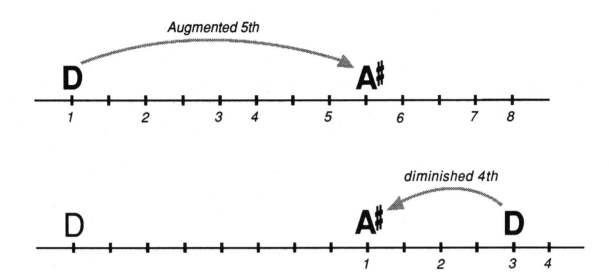

Figure 2-36

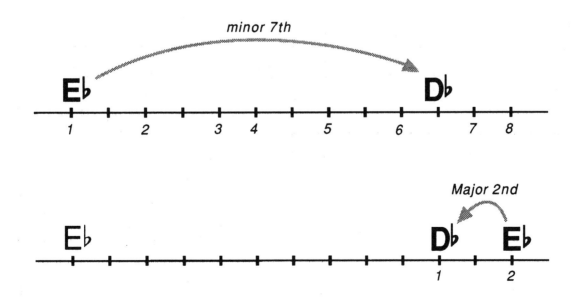

MAJOR SCALES

MAJOR SCALE	1	2	3	4	5	6	7	8
C	C	D	E	F	G	A	B	C
G	G	A	B	C	D	E	F#	G
D	D	E	F#	G	A	B	C#	D
A	A	B	C#	D	E	F#	G#	A
E	E	F#	G#	A	B	C#	D#	E
B	B	C#	D#	E	F#	G#	A#	B
Cb	Cb	Db	Eb	Fb	Gb	Ab	Bb	Cb
F#	F#	G#	A#	B	C#	D#	E#	F#
Gb	Gb	Ab	Bb	Cb	Db	Eb	F	Gb
C#	C#	D#	E#	F#	G#	A#	B#	C#
Db	Db	Eb	F	Gb	Ab	Bb	C	Db
Ab	Ab	Bb	C	Db	Eb	F	G	Ab
Eb	Eb	F	G	Ab	Bb	C	D	Eb
Bb	Bb	C	D	Eb	F	G	A	Bb
F	F	G	A	Bb	C	D	E	F

(Rows B through Db are labeled "Enharmonic Scales")

TEST YOURSELF
CHAPTER 2

1. Write the pattern of half and whole steps that make up the major scale.

   ____ ____ ____ ____ ____ ____ ____

2. How many tones are in a major scale?

   _____

3. Name the first tone of the B♭ major scale. _____

4. Name the eighth tone of the C♯ major scale.

   _____

5. The name of the first scale tone is the _____.

6. The name given to the interval of an eighth is a(n) _____.

7. Spell a B major scale.

   ____ ____ ____ ____ ____ ____ ____ ____

8. Spell a C♭ major scale.

   ____ ____ ____ ____ ____ ____ ____ ____

9. Name these intervals:
   G ascending to B♭:   _____

   D♭ ascending to C: _____

   A♯ ascending to A♯:   _____

   B♭ ascending to F♭:   _____

   C ascending to F♯:   _____

   E♭ ascending to B: _____

10. Fill in the missing letter-name:

    F ascending to _____ is a major 2nd.

    G♭ ascending to _____ is a perfect 4th.

    A ascending to _____ is a major 3rd.

    A ascending to _____ is a diminished 4th.

    B ascending to _____ is an augmented 2nd.

    B ascending to _____ is a minor 3rd.

ANSWERS
TEST YOURSELF
CHAPTER 2

1.   W   W   H   W   W   W   H

2.   8

3.   B♭

4.   C♯

5.   Tonic

6.   Octave

7.   B   C♯   D♯   E   F♯   G♯   A♯   B

8.   C♭   D♭   E♭   F♭   G♭   A♭   B♭   C♭

9.   Minor 3rd
       Major 7th
       Perfect Octave
       Diminished 5th
       Augmented 4th
       Augmented 5th

10.   G
       C♭
       C♯
       D♭
       C✕
       D

CHAPTER 3
CHORD CONSTRUCTION

Chord Basics

A *Chord* is defined as three or more unique (different) tones sounding simultaneously.

A *Triad* is a three tone chord built by intervals of a 3rd from tone to tone. A triad is a chord, but every chord is *not* necessarily a triad.

Triadic, or *tertian*, harmony describes chords built from the *root* upward in intervals of a 3rd from one tone to the next. A *root* is the tone a chord is built upon.[1] For example, a "C major" chord is a major chord whose root is "C"; the other remaining chord tones are built upon the root. All the chords described in this chapter are of a tertian nature.

There are four basic triads in tertian harmony: major, minor, augmented and diminished. These triads either stand alone, or form the foundation for larger chords.

As each of these four chords is defined, the major scale is used as a guide and each chord tone is defined in relation to its root. In addition, some of the most common suffixes (short-hand abbreviations) are given as well.

1.   Major Triad

Figure 3-1

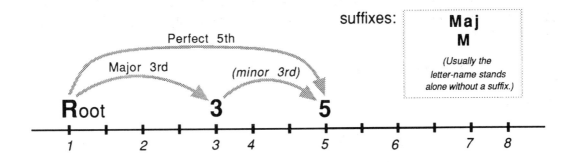

In Figure 3-1 we see that a major triad consists of an ascending major 3rd interval and an ascending perfect 5th interval from the root. Therefore, a C major chord, for example, is spelled C E G.

---

1   "Tonic" is used in reference to scales and intervals; "Root" is used in reference to chords and chord arpeggios.

2.   Minor Triad

Figure 3-2

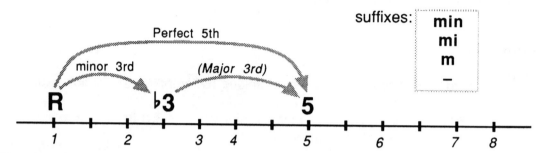

In Figure 3-2 we see the difference between a major and minor triad is the interval of a minor 3rd from the root to 3rd scale degree. For example, a "C minor" chord is, therefore, C E♭ G.

3.   Augmented Triad

Figure 3-3

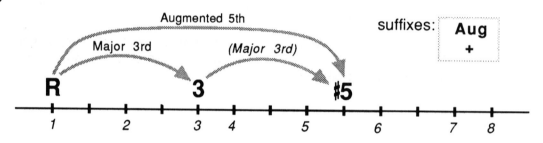

In Figure 3-3 we see the difference between a major and augmented triad is the interval of an augmented 5th from the root to the 5th scale degree. (A "C augmented" chord is spelled C E G♯.)

4.   Diminished Triad

Figure 3-4

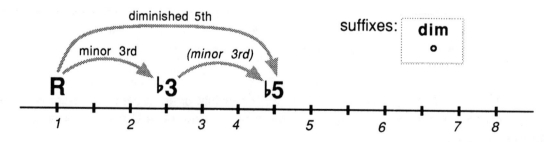

In Figure 3-4 we see the difference between a minor and diminished triad is the interval of a diminished 5th, or tritone, from the root to 5th scale degree. Notice the minor 3rd interval from tone to tone. (A "C diminished" chord is spelled C E♭ G♭).

Figure 3-5 summarizes these four basic triads and their suffixes.

Figure 3-5

Chord Name	Triad Type	Chord Content			Chord Suffixes
Major	Major	R	3	5	Maj *or* M *(usually the letter-name stands alone, without a suffix)*
Minor	Minor	R	♭3	5	min *or* mi *or* m *or* −
Augmented	Augmented	R	3	♯5	aug *or* +
Diminished	Diminished	R	♭3	♭5	dim *or* °

An alteration of the augmented (or diminished ?) triad is the chord containing R 3 ♭5 named with the suffix "flat five" (♭5). This is not a foundational triad in "traditional" music theory, yet this *altered* chord is sometimes found in popular music.

Chord Inversions

While a chord's content remains true to its name (i.e. a chord named major contains R 3 5, a chord named minor contains R ♭3 5 etc...), sometimes chords are inverted. In other words, sometimes the lowest sounding chord tone may be something other than the root. Specifically, a chord may appear several different ways:

a) *Root position*, with the root as the lowest sounding tone;

b) *First inversion*, with the 3rd as the lowest sounding tone;

c) *Second inversion*, with the 5th as the lowest sounding tone.

Larger chords with additional tones are inverted in a like manner, with the possibility of creating a 3rd inversion or greater. Notice every chord inversion is defined *only* by the *lowest sounding chord tone*, regardless of both the order of the remaining tones and the possible duplication of any chord tone.

When reading or writing chords in "letter-name/suffix" form, be aware of the following practices:

a) a chord in root position appears as simply a letter-name followed by a suffix describing the chord type (eg. Cm, F#+, G∘, or B♭ [no suffix necessary for Major chords] etc...);

b) a first inversion B♭ major chord, for example, is written $B♭/D$, meaning a B♭ major chord with D (or the 3rd) as the lowest sounding tone; and likewise,

c) a second inversion C minor chord is written Cm/G , meaning a C minor chord with G (or the 5th) as the lowest sounding tone.

Notice the augmented triad in Figure 3-3 has a major 3rd interval from tone to tone dividing the octave into three equal parts (major 3rds). Because of this unique characteristic, as the augmented chord is inverted, the intervals between tones remains constant. Consequently, any chord tone may be considered the root. For example, a C augmented chord spelled C, E, G# can be inverted as E, G#, C and G#, C, E, yet the interval from tone to tone is always a major 3rd as in root position. Therefore, each inversion of any augmented triad may be considered another root position augmented triad named by its lowest sounding tone. For example, the above inversions of the C+ triad may be named E+ and G#+, respectively.

7th Chords

A seventh chord consists of one of the four basic triads (major, minor, augmented, diminished) with the addition of the 7th scale degree (i.e. the addition of another scale degree a 3rd above the 5th). Figures 3-6 though 3-13 comprise the most common chords of this type.

Figure 3-6

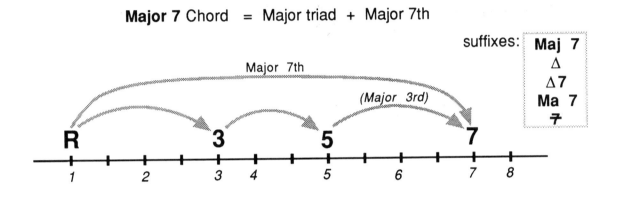

Major 7 Chord = Major triad + Major 7th

suffixes: **Maj 7**
Δ
Δ7
Ma 7
7

Figure 3-7

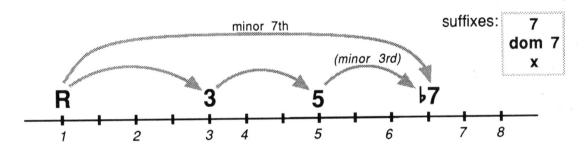

7 or **"Dominant" 7** Chord = Major triad + minor 7th

suffixes: **7**
dom 7
X

Most often the suffix used for this chord is simply "7" by itself. Remember, this suffix implies a ♭7 (*minor 7th*) scale degree added to the root, not a major 7th.

Note: The term "Dominant" refers to a chord's <u>function</u> and/or position in the context of a key or chord progression and should not necessarily be used to describe a chord's content, though it is used in many cases in this book and elsewhere for greater clarity to help distinguish this chord from other 7th chords.

Figure 3-8

minor/Major 7 Chord = minor triad + Major 7th

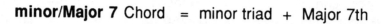
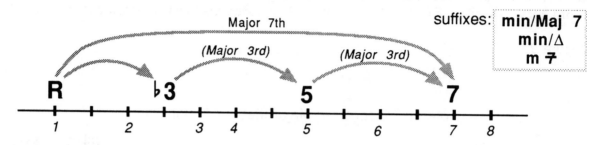

suffixes: **min/Maj 7**
min/△
m 7̄

Notice the interval of a major 3rd between the 3rd, 5th and 7th degree. These intervals give this chord a strong "augmented" sound.

Figure 3-9

minor 7 Chord = minor triad + minor 7th

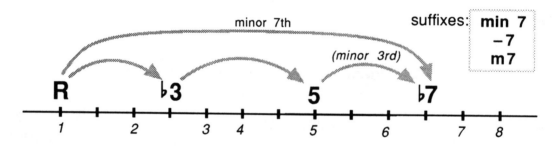

suffixes: **min 7**
−7
m7

Figure 3-10

Major 7, ♯5 Chord = Augmented triad + Major 7th

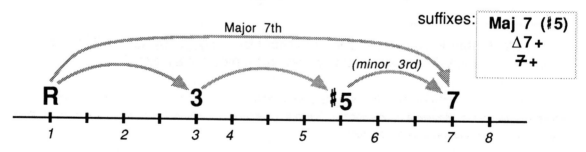

suffixes: **Maj 7 (♯5)**
△7+
7̄+

Figure 3-11

Augmented 7 or **7 (♯5)** Chord   = Augmented triad + minor 7th

suffixes: **aug 7**
7(♯5)
7 +
+7

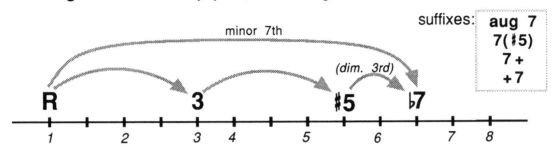

Figure 3-12

minor 7 (♭5) or **half diminished 7** Chord   = diminished triad + minor 7th

suffixes: **–7(♭5)**
m7(♭5)
ø 7

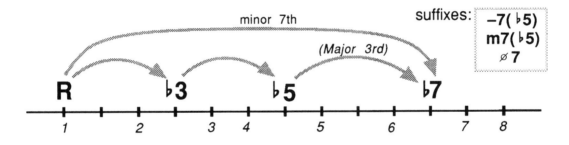

Figure 3-13

diminished 7 Chord   = diminished triad + diminished 7th

suffixes: **dim 7**
○7

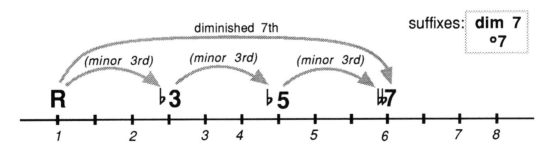

The ○7 chord is special because, like the augmented chord, any tone may be considered, or perceived as, the root because the interval of a minor 3rd remains constant from tone to tone throughout all its inversions (eg. C○7 = E♭○7 = G♭○7 = A○7). This chord is viewed by some as a diminished triad with an added major 6th interval (written as dim. 6 or ○6). Be prepared to find both, though "○7" is more popular.

Table 3-14 summarizes these chords and some of their more popular suffixes.

Table 3-14

Chord Name	Basic Triad Type	Type of 7th Interval	Chord Content				Chord Suffixes
Major seven	Major	Major	R	3	5	7	$\overline{7}$, $\Delta 7$, Δ, Maj. 7
seven or "Dominant" seven	Major	minor	R	3	5	♭7	7, Dom. 7, x
minor, Major seven	minor	Major	R	♭3	5	7	m/Maj. 7, m $\overline{7}$
minor seven	minor	minor	R	♭3	5	♭7	–7, m7
Major seven, sharp five	Augmented	Major	R	3	♯5	7	+$\overline{7}$, $\overline{7}$+, $\overline{7}$(♯5), Maj.7(♯5), $\Delta 7$+
seven, sharp five - or - Augmented seven	Augmented	minor	R	3	♯5	♭7	+7, 7+, Dom. 7(♯5), Dom.7+
minor seven, flat five - or - half diminished seven	diminished	minor	R	♭3	♭5	♭7	–7(♭5), ∅7, m7(♭5)
diminished seven	diminished	diminished	R	♭3	♭5	♭♭7	°7, dim. 7

★★★ **Note:** *Beginning students are advised to skip to Chapter 4 at this point in the book, then to return to this chapter prior to advancing past page 117 in Chapter 6.*

9th, 11th and 13th Chords

Ninth, eleventh and thirteenth chords are created by adding additional intervals of 3rds above the 7th, called *extensions*.

Figure 3-15

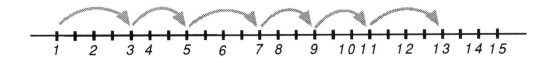

Any chord labelled as a 9, 11 or 13 implies the presence of *all* preceding, or lesser, chord tones. For example, any chord labelled as a 13 implies the presence of the 7th, 9th and 11th scale degrees as well as the 13th, added to one of the four basic triads. In practice, however, one or more of these preceding tones may be omitted.

As you may imagine, the possibility of additional scale degrees produces a myriad of different chord possibilities. This text does *not* attempt to present an exhaustive list of every possible chord or chord suffix, but rather aims to equip the guitarist with all the information necessary to create and interpret chords of virtually any type. Consequently, it is not worthwhile to attempt to memorize every conceivable combination of tones; most importantly however, know and understand the principles governing chord construction and be able to create and interpret chords for yourself!

Many of the common suffixes used to label chords, however, are vague and incomplete, having evolved as a sort of slang or shorthand for musicians because of their wide use in popular and contemporary music, and are not thoroughly descriptive in a theoretical sense. For this reason, familiarity with these suffixes and the chords they represent is necessary.

Let's begin with some major chords.

Figure 3-16

Chord Name	Chord Suffixes	Chord Content						
Major 9	~~9~~ or Maj. 9	R	3	5	7	9		
Major 9 (♯11)	~~9~~ (♯11) or Maj. 9 (♯11)	R	3	5	7	9	♯11	
Major 13	~~13~~ or Maj. 13	R	3	5	7	9	(11)	13
Major 13 (♯11)	Maj. 13 (♯11) or ~~13~~ (♯11)	R	3	5	7	9	♯11	13

Notice the 11th scale degree is crossed out in the major 13 chord. This is because it is usually omitted for its dissonant relation to the 3rd scale degree. If the 11th scale degree is included in a major 13 chord, it will usually be raised a half step, giving us the major 13 (#11) chord. This is also the reason for omitting a major 11 chord from this table and using a major 9(#11) chord instead.

> You may have also noticed there are seven chord tones in a 13 type chord, but only six strings on your guitar. One of these tones must be omitted. Consequently, a perfect 5th scale degree is the first choice in any situation because it is the least colorful chord tone and, if included, can even detract from a chord's character. (This is a reason keyboard players frequently omit this chord tone as well, even though they can physically play it.) The root is the second choice for omission having the next least color.

Let's take a look at some "dominant" type chords.

Figure 3-17

Chord Name	Chord Suffixes	Chord Contents						
Nine	9 *or* dom 9	R	3	5	♭7	9		
Nine, (#11) *or* aug11	9(#11) *or* +11	R	3	5	♭7	9	#11	
Eleven	11	R	(3)	5	♭7	9	11	
Thirteen	13	R	3	5	♭7	9	(11)	13
Thirteen, (#11)	13 (#11)	R	3	5	♭7	9	#11	13

Most importantly, notice that each of these chord names and their symbols implies a ♭7 scale degree, even though this is not overtly stated in either the chord name or suffix.

Looking at the chords in Figure 3-17, again we see the practice of either omitting the 11th (because of its dissonance with the 3rd) or raising it a half step. The "eleven" chord, however, is of special interest because in everyday use the *3rd* is removed. In actuality, the 3rd is more accurately considered *raised* a half tone, giving us the chord called 9sus4 (to be discussed shortly); in this case, the raised 3rd, i.e. the 4th, is the same tone as the 11th, hence the name 9sus4, *not* "11". The "11" suffix is consequently used more frequently by musicians for its brevity, not accuracy. This popular chord may appear a few different ways. Let's say, for example, we have a C11 chord spelled C G B♭ D F. This chord may also be written as G−7/C, that is G−7 with C as the lowest sounding tone. Another variation of this C11 chord is B♭/C, i.e. a B♭ chord with C as the lowest sounding tone. This chord omits the 5th (G) of the C11 chord as well as the 3rd, and is more popular than the others for guitarists because it is easily executed yet captures the essential sound of an "11" chord.

> Any chord with an omitted 3rd takes on an ambiguous nature since it may be perceived as either major or minor. The "11" chord in Figure 3-17 shown in the "dominant" chord group is almost identical to the "minor 11" chord in Figure 3-18 except for the 3rd. Consequently, this chord (without its 3rd) may be perceived as major or minor depending on its musical context.

Also, the 13 chord in everyday use does not contain the 11th scale degree (R 3 5 ♭7 9 13). Consequently, a more accurate name for this chord is 9add13 or 9add6 (to be discussed shortly). If an 11th scale degree appears in a 13 chord, it will most likely be a ♯11, giving us the chord called 13(♯11). Often times, the 9th as well as the 11th factors are omitted from the 13 chord by guitarists in particular. In this case, a more accurate name is 7add13 or 7add6 (sometimes written: 7/6). Again, "13" is an example of a suffix used for its brevity, not accuracy.

Finally, let's look at some minor chords. (Augmented and diminished chords will be discussed with altered chords.)

Figure 3-18

Chord Name	Chord Suffixes	Chord Content					
minor/Maj 9	m/Maj 9 *or* m⊖	R	♭3	5	7	9	
minor /Maj 9(♯11)	m/Maj 9(♯11) *or* m⊖ (♯11)	R	♭3	5	7	9	♯11
minor 9(♭5)	−9(♭5) *or* m9(♭5)	R	♭3	♭5	♭7	9	
minor 9	−9 *or* m9 *or* mi9	R	♭3	5	♭7	9	
minor 11	−11 *or* m11 *or* mi11	R	♭3	5	♭7	9	11
minor 9 (♯11)	−9 (♯11) *or* m9(♯11)	R	♭3	5	♭7	9	♯11

Even though 13 chords are not included here since they are not used as frequently, realize the possibility of adding this scale degree to any of these chords.

Because there is less tension between the minor 3rd and perfect (natural) 11th, the 11th scale degree is more at home here.

Suspended Chords

A suspended chord is formed by temporarily replacing the 3rd scale degree with the 4th (suspended 4), or sometimes with the 2nd (suspended 2), or sometimes both (suspended 4 and 2) before resolving this suspended tone(s) back to the 3rd. This isn't quite a "theory book" definition, yet it better serves our purposes.

Sometimes chords labelled as "suspended" do not resolve their suspended tone and may more accurately be understood as another type of chord (chords built by 4ths, not 3rds, discussed in Chapter 7; or chords with added tones), yet, for practical purposes, the "suspended" label may work best.

Figure 3-19 shows the most common suspended chords.

Figure 3-19

Chord Name	Chord Suffixes	Chord Content					
suspended 2	sus 2	R	2	5			
suspended 4	sus 4 *or* sus	R		4 5			
suspended 4 and 2	sus $\frac{4}{2}$	R	2	4 5			
seven, suspended 4	7 sus 4	R		4 5	♭7		
nine, suspended 4	9 sus 4	R		4 5	♭7	9	
thirteen, suspended 4	13 sus 4	R		4 5	♭7	9	13

As we already learned in Chapter 2, the 4th and 11th scale degrees have the same letter-name (as do the 2nd and 9th, and 6th and 13th). With this in mind, analyze the chord content of the 9 sus 4 and 11 chords (already discussed on page 36).

Figure 3-20

Chord Suffixes	Chord Content				
9 sus 4	R	4 5	♭7	9	
11	R	5	♭7	9	11

Because the 11 chord played most often in contemporary music lacks a 3rd, this chord is more accurately called 9 sus 4. Most musicians, however, use the 11 chord label for R 5 ♭7 9 11 since it is faster to write and other musicians know to omit the 3rd by practice.

Also worth mentioning, the 13 sus 4 chord, C13 sus 4 for example, may appear as B♭Maj7/C. This is similar to the alternate use of G-7/C or B♭/C for C 9 sus 4. [2]

---

[2] See **Chord Plurality**, Chapter 6.

Chords with Added Tones

Some chords have an irregular construction. While beginning with a tertian foundation consisting of intervals of consecutive 3rds (in root position), sometimes other tones are simply added to a tertian chord. Some frequently added tones are the 9th (or 2nd), 11th (or 4th) and 6th (or 13th). Here is a table containing the most popular chords.

Figure 3-21

Chord Name	Chord Suffixes	Chord Content				
six *or* Major six	6 *or* Maj.6	R	3	5 6		
minor six	m6 *or* −6	R	♭3	5 6		
six add 9 *or* six, nine	$\frac{9}{6}$ *or* $\frac{6}{9}$	R	3	5 6	9	
minor six add nine	m$\frac{9}{6}$ *or* −$\frac{6}{9}$	R	♭3	5 6	9	
minor 7 add 11	−7 add11	R	♭3	5	♭7	11
minor 7 add 4	−7 add4	R	♭3 4 5		♭7	
add nine	add9	R	3	5	9	
Two *or* add two	2 *or* add2	R 2 3		5		

You are likely to come across all these chords at some time or another. Please note that the "add 9" and "2" chords, and the "add 11" and "add 4" chords, for all intents and purposes, are identical.

Compare the "add 9" or "2" chord to both the "sus 2" and "9" chords in Figure 3-24. Be sure you know the differences between each of these chords.

Figure 3-22

Chord Suffixes	Chord Content				
add9	R	3	5		9
2	R	2 3	5		
sus2	R	2	5		
9 *or* dom 9	R	3	5	♭7	9

Chords with an added tone as the lowest sounding voice represent a special type of chord. A chord such as $B\flat/D$ merely represents a $B\flat$ chord in first inversion with "D" (the 3rd) as the lowest sounding tone, as mentioned earlier in this chapter. Similarly, A/E represents an "A" chord in second inversion with "E" (the 5th) as the lowest sounding tone. However, a chord like $B\flat/C$, mentioned in the paragraphs following Figure 3-17, may be perceived as a major chord ($B\flat$ Major) with "C" *added* as the lowest sounding tone. "C" may be perceived as an added 2nd or 9th tone since it does not naturally occur in a $B\flat$ chord. Chords of this type, with an added non-chord tone in the lowest sounding voice, are most often perceived with this added tone as the chord *root* because *the lowest sounding tone (or bass) in any harmonic situation most often dominates and defines the harmony.* This is especially true of tones occurring in the lowest register of the guitar or overall musical ensemble. Consequently, $B\flat/C$ is perceived as a C^{11} chord as discussed earlier in this chapter. On the contrary, though a $B\flat 2$ or $B\flat \text{add} 9$ chord contains the exact same tones as $B\flat/C$ (R 3 5 9, that is, $B\flat$ D F C), because "$B\flat$" is the lowest sounding chord tone, "$B\flat$" is perceived as the chord root, *not* "C".

Another example is C/F, that is, a C major chord with "F" as the lowest sounding tone. "F" may be perceived as an added 4th or 11th tone since it does not naturally occur in a C chord. Because "F" is the lowest sounding tone, however, "F" is strongly perceived as the chord root, dominating and defining the harmony. Consequently, C/F is perceived as $F^{Maj9}_{(no\ 3rd)}$, or maybe $F^{Maj7sus2}$.[3]

In yet other situations, a series of chords may progress over a common bass tone, called a *pedal tone.* For example, C, F and G major chords may all progress over a common bass tone of "C". In this instance, the G chord tends to retain its identity in light of its *musical context,* even though when isolated it appears as a chord with an added non-chord tone in its lowest voice. Ultimately and in any event, the way chords are used in the context of a musical setting most often determines how they are individually perceived, interpreted and named.

---

[3] See **Chord Synonyms,** Chapter 6.

Altered Chords

In general, chords containing a $\flat 5$ ($\sharp 11$), $\sharp 5$ ($\flat 13$), $\flat 9$ and/or $\sharp 9$ are considered *altered* chords, though the "dominant" 7 type (containing a major 3rd and a minor 7th) are the most common variety. [4] Extended augmented and diminished chords are not necessarily considered altered chords depending on their context, however, since their construction and naming is identical, or at least similar, to other extended altered chords they are mentioned in this category.

The names of these chords are usually as descriptive as they need to be so you'll know how the chord is built. For example, a $+7(\flat 9)$ chord is constructed R 3 $\sharp 5$ $\flat 7$ $\flat 9$, or a $7\left(\substack{\sharp 9 \\ \flat 5}\right)$ chord is constructed R 3 $\flat 5$ $\flat 7$ $\sharp 9$.

Sometimes, the "+" symbol may be used to describe a $\sharp 9$ or $\sharp 11$ scale degree as in $C^7(+9)$ or $C^{13}(+11)$. Likewise, the "– " symbol may be used to describe a $\flat 5$ or $\flat 9$ scale degree as in $C^7(-5)$ or $C7\left(\substack{13 \\ -9}\right)$. This author prefers to use the "+" symbol to refer exclusively to a $\sharp 5$ and the "– " symbol to refer exclusively to a $\flat 3$ to avoid confusion.

Be aware that two different altered interval numbers may refer to the same sounding chord tone. For example, a $\flat 5$ refers to the same sounding chord tone as a $\sharp 11$, and a $\sharp 5$ refers to the same sounding chord tone as a $\flat 13$. Remember, the highest numbered chord tone implies the presence of *all* preceding, or lesser, chord tones. For example, the chord containing C E $G\flat$ $B\flat$ and $D\flat$ is best called a $C^7\left(\substack{\flat 9 \\ \flat 5}\right)$ than a $C^7\left(\substack{\sharp 11 \\ \flat 5}\right)$ since calling the $G\flat$ chord tone a $\sharp 11$ (or $F\sharp$) infers a 5th (G) is also present. Similarly, a chord containing C E $G\flat$ $G\sharp$ $B\flat$ and $D\flat$ is best called a $C^{+7}(\sharp 11)$ rather than a $C^7\left(\substack{\flat 13 \\ \sharp 11}\right)$ or $C^7\left(\substack{\flat 13 \\ \flat 5}\right)$.
As another example, the chord containing C $D\flat$ $D\sharp$ E G and $B\flat$ is best called $C^7\left(\substack{\sharp 9 \\ \flat 9}\right)$ and probably not anything else. However, the chord containing C $D\flat$ $D\sharp$ E $G\sharp$ and $B\flat$ may be called $C^{+7}\left(\substack{\sharp 9 \\ \flat 9}\right)$ or rather $C^{altered}$ ($C^{alt.}$) as this suffix is popular for chords with multiple alterations.

Unfortunately, naming chord suffixes is seldom consistent and often varies from person to person. Be prepared to interpret altered chord suffixes differently depending on the composer and musical context. Many liberties are taken by jazz musicians when performing "dominant" 7 chords, altered chords in particular, or any other chord for that matter.

---

[4]   Theoretically speaking, only chords containing *nondiatonic* scale tones are considered altered chords. This *may* be somewhat understood by the end of this text, however, more music theory beyond the scope of this book needs explaining to truly understand this statement. Nevertheless, the information presented in this text is sufficient for understanding and interpreting altered chord construction without a detailed theoretical discourse.

CHAPTER 3
TEST YOURSELF

1. A _____ is _____ or more unique tones sounding simultaneously.

2. A _____ is a three tone _____ built by intervals of a 3rd from tone to tone.

3. Name the four basic types of triads.

    _____ _____ _____ _____

4. Name the root of a D♭ diminished triad.

    _____

5. Spell the following chords:

    a) D♭ major _____

    b) G♯ minor _____

    c) B aug. _____

    d) C♯ dim. _____

6. C F A are the tones (from lowest to highest sounding) of an F major chord in _____ inversion.

7. Name these chords and their position or inversion.
    (*Tones are written from lowest to highest sounding*)

	Chord	**Position**
Eg. A♭ C E♭	A♭ major	root position
a) F♯ A♯ C♯	_____	_____
b) B♭ E♭ G	_____	_____
c) E G♯ C♯	_____	_____
d) A D F	_____	_____
e) B♭ E G	_____	_____
f) D F♯ A♯	_____	_____
g) G B♭ D♭	_____	_____
h) G B E	_____	_____

8.   Spell these chords:

a) D^7

b) Bb^{-7}

c) $E\circ 7$

d) Ab Maj.7

e) C^{+7}

f) $F\sharp^7$

g) Bm/Maj.7

h) F Maj.7($\sharp$5)

i) A^{-7}

j) D Maj.7

9.   Name the chords containing these tones (There may be more than one correct answer):

a) C E G Bb D

b) D F$\sharp$ A C$\sharp$ E B

c) Eb Gb Bb Db F

d) F Bb C Eb G D

e) Gb Bb Db Eb Ab

f) G$\sharp$ B$\sharp$ D$\sharp$ F$\sharp$ A A$\sharp$ D

g) A C$\sharp$ E G B F$\sharp$

h) Bb F Ab C Eb

i) C$\sharp$ E$\sharp$ G$\sharp$ D$\sharp$

j) Db F Ab Cb Eb F$\times$ Bb

k) Eb F Bb

l) F A C G

m) Gb Bb Db Fb Ab

n) Ab C Eb Gb $B\flat\flat$

o) A D E G

ANSWERS
SELF TEST
CHAPTER 3

1.   Chord, three

2.   Triad, chord

3.   Major, Minor, Augmented, Diminished

4.   D♭

5.   a) D♭:   D♭ F A♭
     b) G♯m: G♯ B D♯
     c) B aug: B D♯ G
     d) C♯ dim: C♯ E G

6.   Second

7.   a) F♯ major   root pos.
     b) E♭ major   2nd inv.
     c) C♯ minor   1st inv.
     d) D minor   2nd inv.
     e) E dim   2nd inv.
     f) D +   root pos.
     g) G dim   root pos.
     h) E minor   1st inv.

8.   a) D F♯ A C   f) F♯ A♯ C♯ E
     b) B♭ D♭ F A♭   g) B D F♯ A♯
     c) E G B♭ D♭   h) F A C♯ E
     d) A♭ C E♭ G   i) A C E G
     e) C E G♯ B♭   j) D F♯ A C♯

9.   a) C^9 i) $C♯^2$

     b) $D \text{ Maj}^{13}$ j) $D♭^7$

     c) $E♭^{-11}$ k) $E♭\text{ sus}2$

     d) $F^{13}\text{sus}4$ l) F^2 or $_{\text{add}9}$

     e) G♭   m) $G♭^9$

     f) $G♯^{\text{alt.}}$ n) $A♭^{7(♭9)}$

     g) A^{13} o) $A^7\text{sus}4$

     h) $B♭^{11}$

CHAPTER 4
ESSENTIAL FINGERBOARD PATTERNS

The guitarists ability to command his instrument and express his inner musical creativity through his instrument, is directly proportional to the extent he comprehends and can make use of the guitar's unique fingerboard patterns. These patterns are extremely important!

The fact that the standard guitar's six strings are tuned primarily in perfect 4ths (with one exception) is the basis for these unique patterns. The tuning pattern in terms of intervals is as follows:

the 5th string (A) is tuned a perfect 4th above the 6th string (E);

the 4th string (D) is tuned a perfect 4th above the 5th string (A);

the 3rd string (G) is tuned a perfect 4th above the 4th string (D);

the 2nd string (B) is tuned a major 3rd above the 3rd string (G), this is the exception; and,

the 1st string (E) is tuned a perfect 4th above the 2nd string (B).

Unison Patterns

Because of the nature of the guitar's tuning, there is duplication, or overlapping, of identical tones occurring on all strings. When two tones are identical in pitch (sharing the same letter-name), the interval is a (Perfect) Unison. One way you may have discovered unisons already is by trying to tune your guitar using the "string-to-string" method. In other words, using this tuning method, the 5th string (A) for example is tuned to sound identical in pitch, or in perfect unison, to the tone at the 5th fret of the 6th string (A).

Figure 4-1

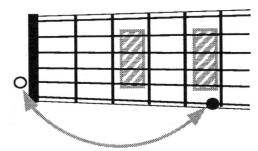

These two tones, at the open 5th string and the 5th fret of the 6th string, are identical in pitch.

Citing an extreme example, let's start with the first open string, or "high E". This tone may be played at five different places on the fingerboard (six different places if you have twenty-four frets);

1) the first string, open, as previously mentioned;
2) the 5th fret of the 2nd string;
3) the 9th fret of the 3rd string;
4) the 14th fret of the 4th string;
5) the 19th fret of the 5th string; and maybe,
6) the 24th fret of the 6th string.

Figure 4-2

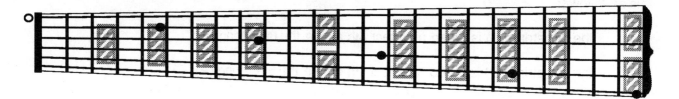

Notice the pattern from string to string. Each tone is five frets apart from the next *except* between the 3rd and 2nd strings, where they are four frets apart. Because of the guitar's tuning, this *"wrinkle"* always occurs when crossing or straddling the 3rd or 2nd strings for *all* patterns on the fingerboard!

Octave Patterns

There are basically two useful octave patterns.

Figure 4-3

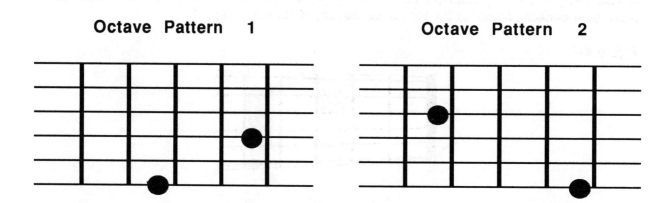

Octave Pattern 1

Octave Pattern 2

In order to work with these octave patterns any further, we need to first learn how patterns transpose (physically move about) on the guitar fingerboard.

Horizontal Transposition (Moving *Along* the Strings)

The simplest way to transpose any pattern on the guitar is to move that pattern horizontally along the strings in either direction keeping all the elements of that pattern in *unchanging relation* to one another. For example, look again at the two octave patterns in Figure 4-3.

The two tones in octave patterns 1 and 2 are an octave apart. If either of these patterns is moved *along* the strings (horizontally up or down the fingerboard) maintaining the same physical relationship of both tones, the interval remains an octave (both tones always have the same letter-name).

Figure 4-4

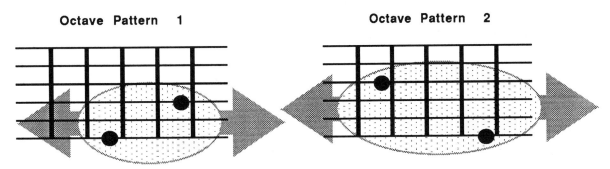

Octave Pattern 1   **Octave Pattern 2**

Either of these patterns is an octave played at any fret on the fingerboard. (Both tones will always have the same letter name). The pattern may move and, consequently, the letter-name will change, but the interval of an octave does not change.

Vertical Transposition (Moving *Across* the Strings)

A pattern may also be transposed by moving it vertically across the strings.

Figure 4-5

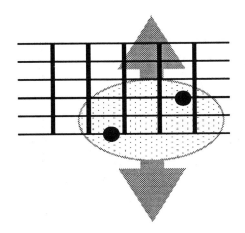 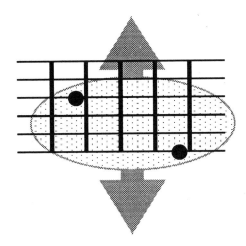

This type of movement across the strings is a little trickier because of the previously mentioned "wrinkle" when crossing or straddling the 3rd or 2nd strings. Watch what happens when moving Octave Pattern 1 from Figure 4-3 in this next example.

Figure 4-6

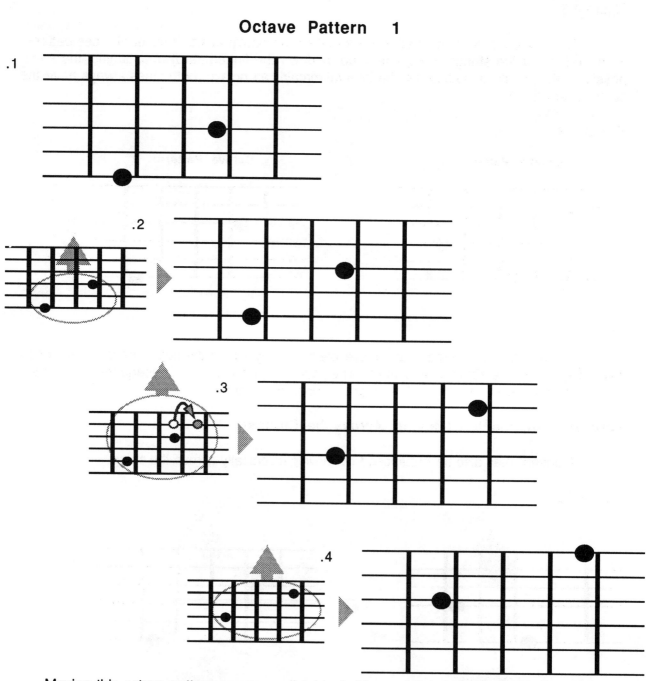

Octave Pattern 1

Moving this octave pattern seems predictable in Figure 4-6.1 to 4-6.2. In Figure 4-6.3, however, we see the "wrinkle" effect the guitar's tuning has on this pattern. The pattern may now look a little different in Figures 4-6.3 and 4-6.4, but the interval of an octave remains the same (both tones have the same letter-name).

Now take a look at Octave Pattern 2 from Figure 4-3 when transposed in the same manner. Notice the same "wrinkle" takes place as this pattern is transposed.

Figure 4-7

Octave Pattern 2

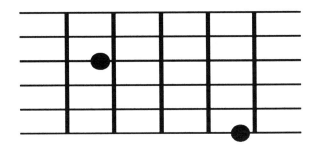

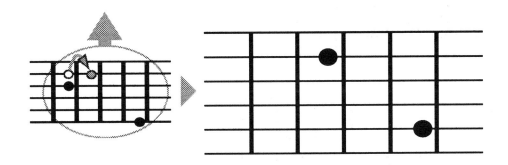

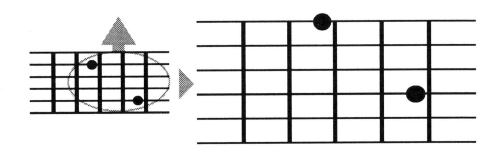

Octave Regions

Figure 4-8 presents basic octave patterns 1 and 2 assembled in the framework of, what we shall call, five octave regions. In some cases, the basic octave patterns are expanded to encompass two octaves within a particular octave region (Regions 1 and 5). The octave patterns assembled into these five octave regions overlap in a cyclical manner across the entire fingerboard.

Figure 4-8

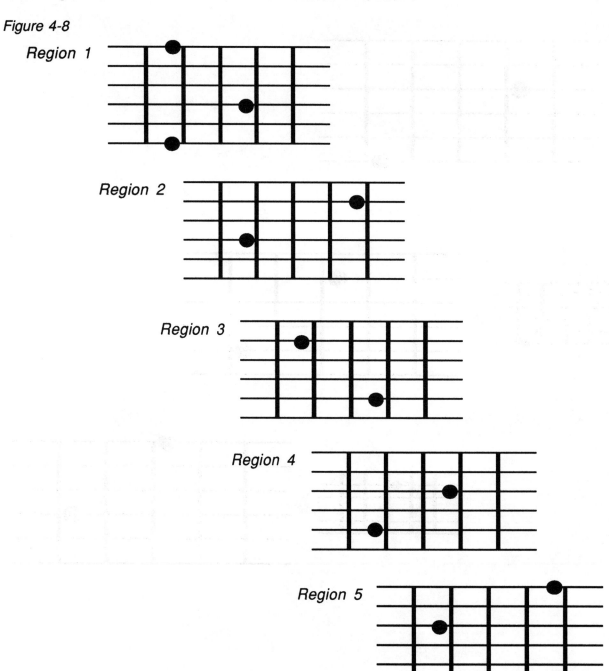

These octave patterns are the "skeleton" that will support all future fingerboard patterns. Consequently, mastering these octave patterns is essential for expert fingerboard navigation!

Figure 4-9 shows how these five regions overlap.

Figure 4-9

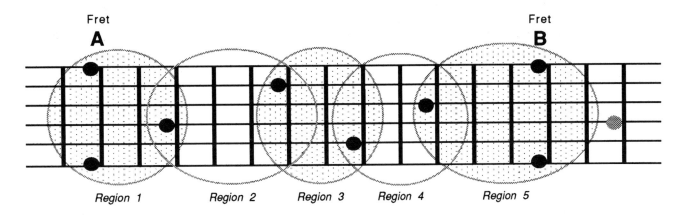

From fret "A" to fret "B" in Figure 4-9 is twelve frets (or one octave on any individual string). Notice the cyclical nature of these patterns as Region 5 and Region 1 overlap at frets "A" and "B".

Remember that because all these tones have the same letter-name, these octave patterns are a great help in finding your place on the fingerboard. Also, recognize that these octave patterns may represent any tone; all you need to do is begin at a tone you know and apply, or assemble, these octave patterns to that tone. For example, if you want to find every E on the guitar (in every octave), all you do is simply select one tone on the guitar that you know is E (the 6th string, open, for example) as a starting place. Then from that tone begin to traverse the fingerboard an octave at a time.

Figure 4-10

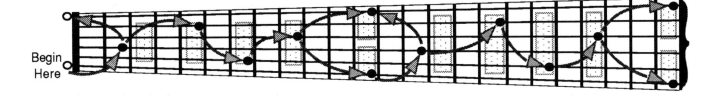

Major Scale Patterns

As explained in Chapter 2, a major scale is a series of eight tones, called scale degrees, adhering to a fixed pattern of half and whole steps from tone to tone, with the eighth scale tone a perfect octave apart from the tonic, or first scale tone. The second essential step to navigating the guitar fingerboard is mastering the major scale in all its patterns and transpositions.

Earlier we described two basic octave patterns as the "skeleton" that will support other fingerboard patterns. There are three basic major scale patterns. The first two basic major scale patterns may be attached to the first octave pattern from Figure 4-3. These patterns are more clearly seen revealing each scale degree by number, with "T" representing the tonic, or first scale degree. [1]

Figure 4-11

Octave Pattern 1

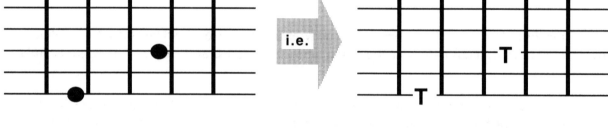

Major Scale Pattern 1   **Major Scale Pattern 2**

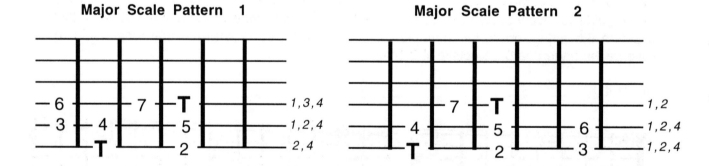

---

*A word about left-hand **fingering**:* In simplest terms, the fingering that works best for you personally is the correct fingering. Through *experience* you'll find a certain fingering more appropriate than another depending upon the physical demands of a particular situation: specifically, how one fingering may lead you into or out of another to your greatest advantage. The fingering indications provided in this text are meant as a guide, especially for the beginner, and are not the only, necessarily correct, choices.

---

[1]   Refer to Appendix 1 if you need help understanding these diagrams.

The third basic major scale pattern may be attached to the second octave pattern from Figure 4-3.

Figure 4-12

Octave Pattern 2

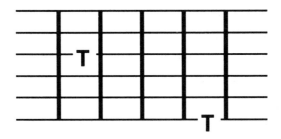

Major Scale Pattern 3

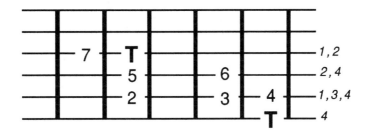

Any one of these major scale patterns may be transposed horizontally along the strings to produce any possible major scale.

Figure 4-13

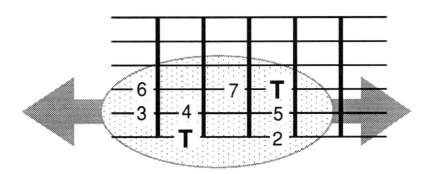

The letter-name of the major scale depends on the letter-name of the tonic.

For example, if we begin the first major scale pattern from Figure 4-11 with the tonic at the 5th fret of the 6th string, we would have an A major scale because the tone at the 5th fret of the 6th string is A.

In the next examples, note the "wrinkle" effect the guitar's tuning has on these major scale patterns when transposing them *vertically* across the strings.

Figure 4-14

Major Scale Pattern 1

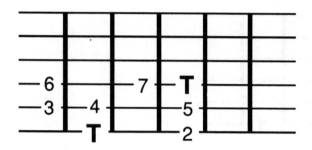

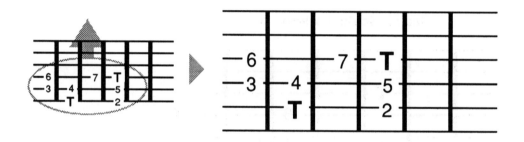

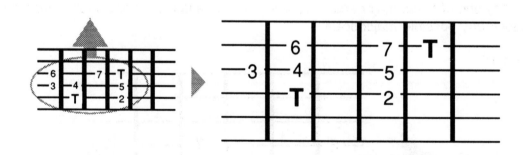

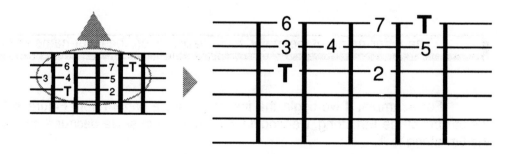

Major Scale Pattern 2

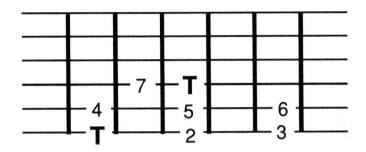

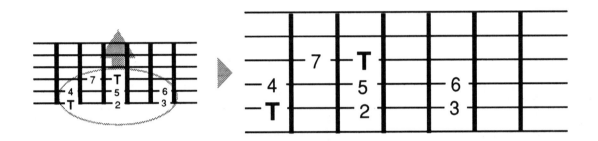

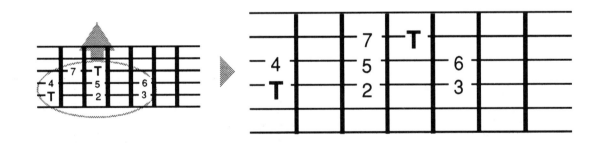

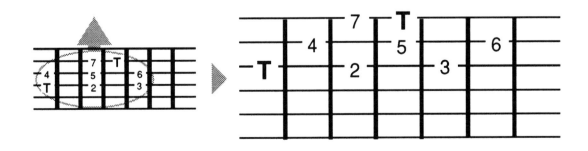

Major Scale Pattern 3

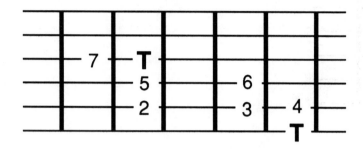

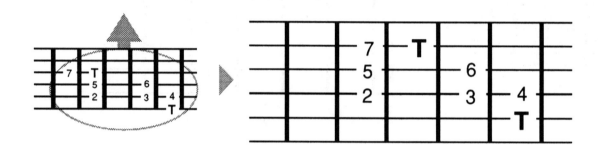

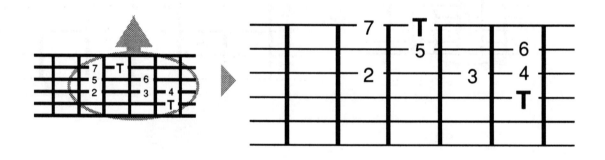

Remember, the moveable nature of patterns on the fingerboard permits any of these patterns to be transposed (moved) horizontally along the strings or vertically across the strings. *That is, no matter where these patterns are moved on the fingerboard, they ALWAYS produce a major scale.*

Now let's attach these scale patterns to each of the five (overlapping) octave regions.

Figure 4-15

Octave Region 1

This is the major scale in the *first octave* of *Octave Region 1.*

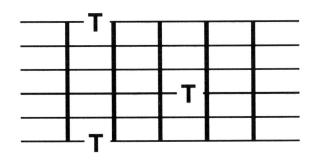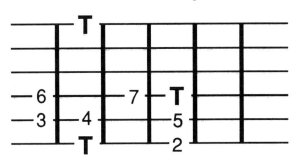

Let's continue this scale through the next octave of Octave Region 1.

Figure 4-16

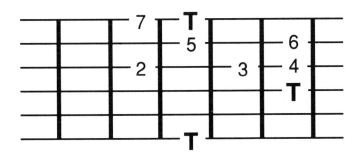

Here's what the major scale looks like through two octaves in the first octave region.

Figure 4-17

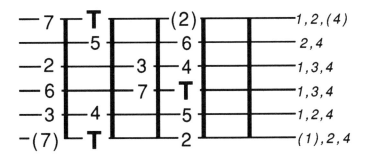

Now let's attach major scale patterns to Octave Region 2.

Figure 4-18

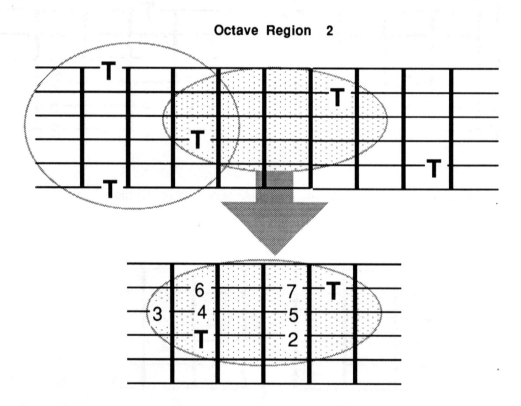

Because the major scale pattern in this octave region occurs on the middle guitar strings, let's extend this pattern to the outer strings, staying within the general four fret span of our pattern in Figure 4-18 for ease of fingering.

Figure 4-19

...*extending upward*

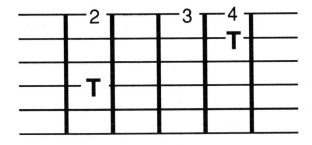

...*extending downward*

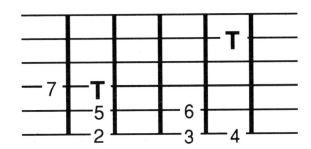

...*all together*

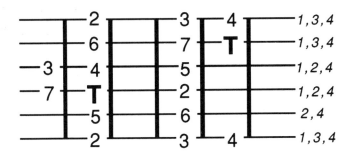

Notice how this scale pattern overlaps with the previous scale pattern in the first octave region.

Figure 4-20

Major Scale Pattern: Ocatave Region 1   Major Scale Pattern: Ocatave Region 2

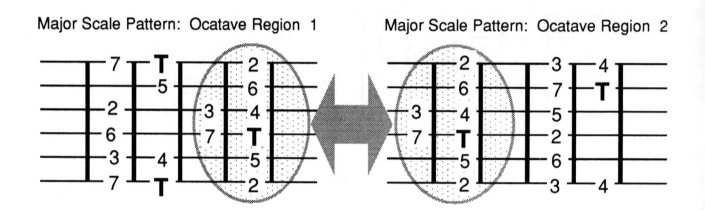

Both Patterns Together

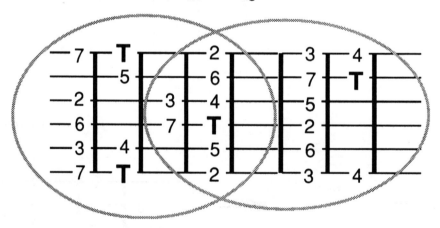

As you may guess, the major scale pattern in the third octave region likewise overlaps the scale pattern in the previous octave region (Octave Region 2), as do all succeeding major scale patterns.

Figure 4-21

Octave Region 3

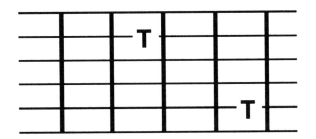 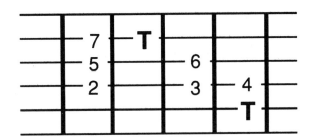

Extending the pattern to the neighboring strings we get:

Figure 4-22

...extending upward

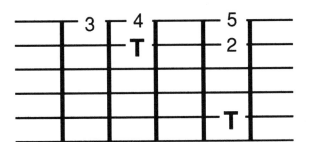

...extending downward

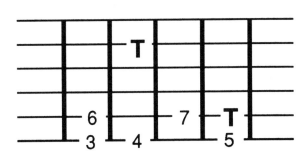

...all together

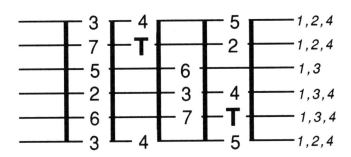

Now for major scale patterns in the remaining octave regions:

Figure 4-23

Octave Region 4

...octave pattern   *...scale pattern*

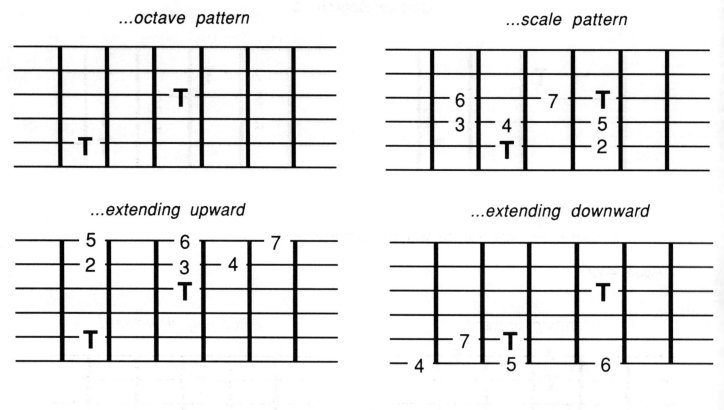

...extending upward   *...extending downward*

...all together

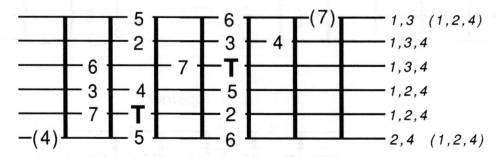

Next,

Figure 4-24

Octave Region 5

...octave pattern   *...scale pattern*

...extending upward   *...extending downward*

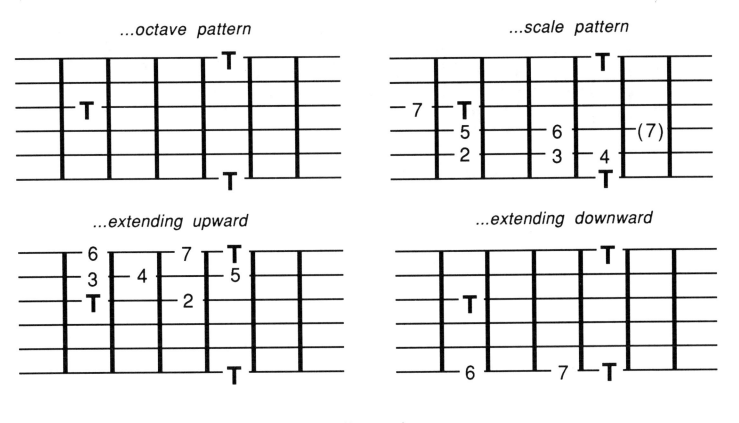

...all together

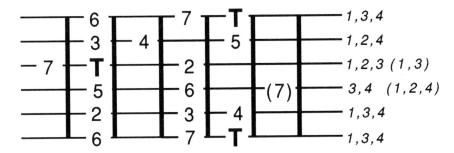

Now let's look at the major scale as it overlaps in all five octave regions. [2]

Figure 4-25

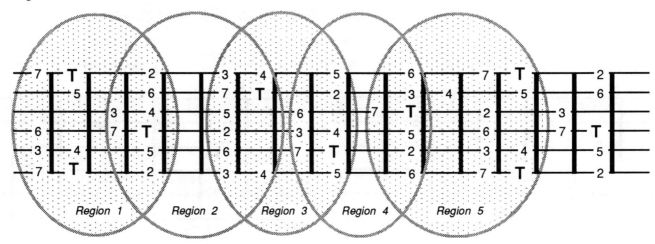

Notice how the 5th and 1st octave regions overlap.

---

[2] These scale patterns in five octave regions are based mostly on Major Scale Patterns 1 and 2 from Figures 4-11 and 4-12. Appendix 3 summarizes these scale patterns in all five octave regions. In addition, for more advanced students, another group of seven overlapping major scale patterns is shown in this appendix based mostly on Major Scale Pattern 2 from Figure 4-11.

Now watch what happens when we take the major scale pattern in the entire first octave region and begin to transpose it vertically across the strings.   (Remember the "wrinkle".)

Figure 4-26

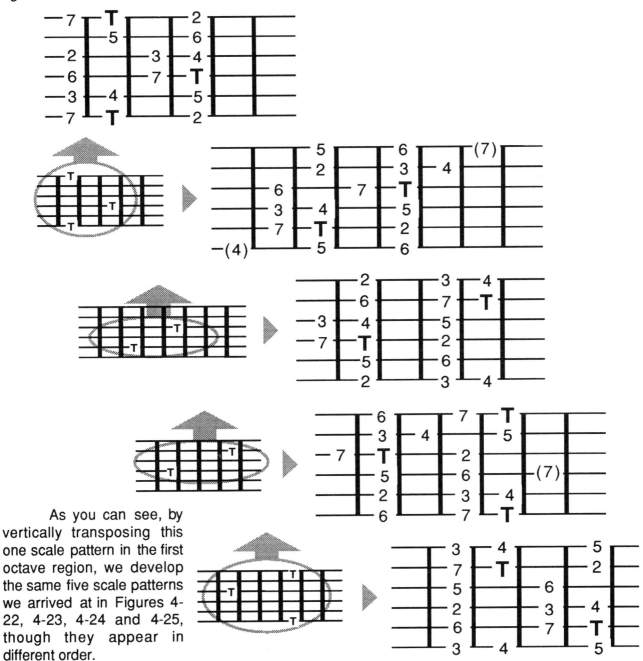

As you can see, by vertically transposing this one scale pattern in the first octave region, we develop the same five scale patterns we arrived at in Figures 4-22, 4-23, 4-24 and 4-25, though they appear in different order.

Conclusion: There are three basic fingerboard patterns of the major scale. These basic major scale patterns may be expanded and assembled into five larger patterns contained within the framework of five octave regions. These larger patterns contained within only five octave regions are the interconnecting "pieces" whereby the major scale may be manipulated across the entire fingerboard!

Intervallic Patterns

By applying our theoretical knowledge of intervals, and dissecting major scale patterns, we will assemble fingerboard patterns for individual intervals.

As we saw before, the interval of a major 2nd may be graphically illustrated as follows.

Figure 4-27

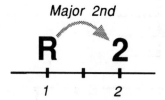

Basic intervallic patterns may be extracted from any of the major scale patterns developed earlier in this chapter, making graphic illustrations of intervals (from Chapter 2) "come alive" as useable guitar fingerboard patterns. Here are some possible major 2nd interval patterns.

Figure 4-28

Major 2nd

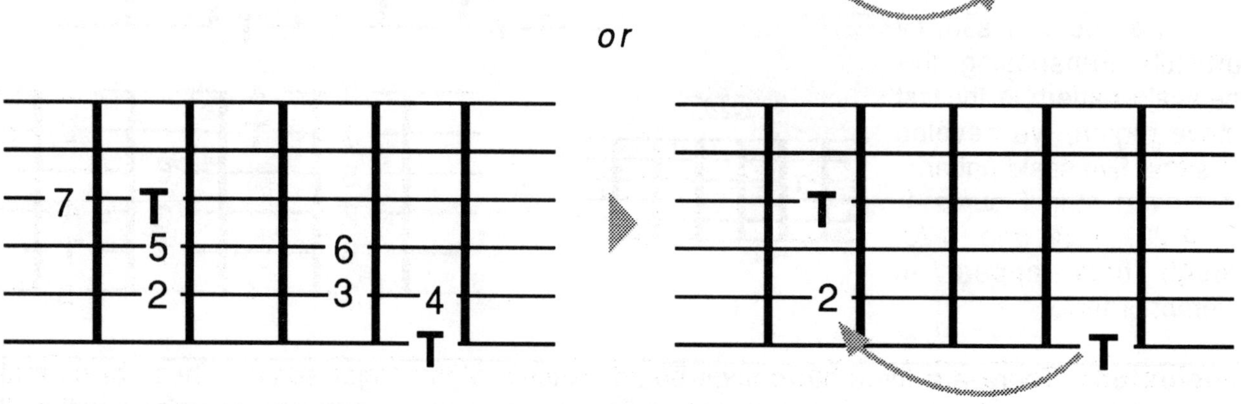

or

Figure 4-29 shows some other intervallic patterns extracted from a major scale pattern. Major Scale Pattern 1 happens to be used for these examples, though any major scale pattern may be used.

Figure 4 -29

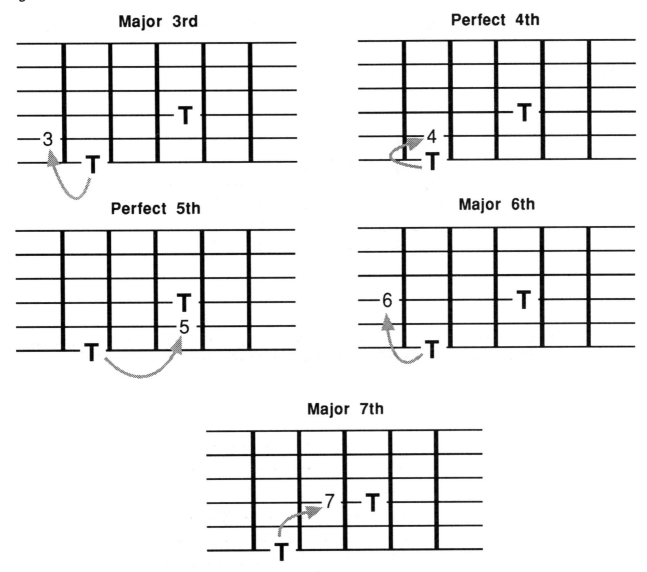

Notice how each interval in the preceding examples is contained within the framework of an octave pattern. Applying the principle of *interval inversions* (from Chapter 2), any desired tone may be attained by the, perhaps shorter, alternate route of an interval's inversion, and not only the direct intervallic route. For example, instead of arriving at the 7th scale tone by the long distance of a major 7th from the tonic, we may:

   a) begin an octave above the tonic and descend the short distance of a minor 2nd, thus arriving at the desired tone;

Figure 4-30

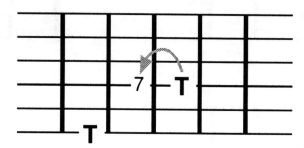

or b) simply descend a minor 2nd from the tonic, though this route places the desired tone outside the original octave pattern an octave below an ascending major 7th.

Figure 4-31

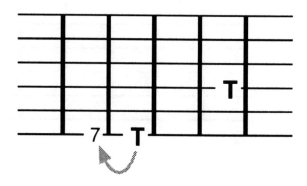

Chapter 2 presented many types of intervals while Chapter 3 applied these intervals to develop many chord formulas. Consequently, presenting a few more of the most common intervallic patterns on the fingerboard is worth while.

Figure 4-32

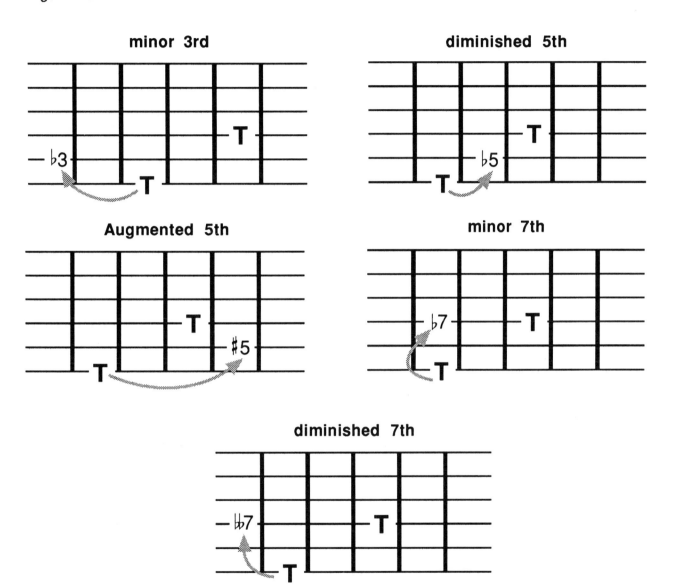

Intervallic fingerboard patterns larger than an octave may be found by simply associating these larger intervals with their *primary octave counter-parts*. Specifically, since the letter-names of the 9th, 11th and 13th intervals are identical to the 2nd, 4th and 6th intervals, respectively, finding these fingerboard patterns is very easy. In these diagrams, notice Octave Region 1 is used since it more readily shows two adjacent octave patterns, though this octave region is certainly not the only place these intervals are found.

Figure 4-33

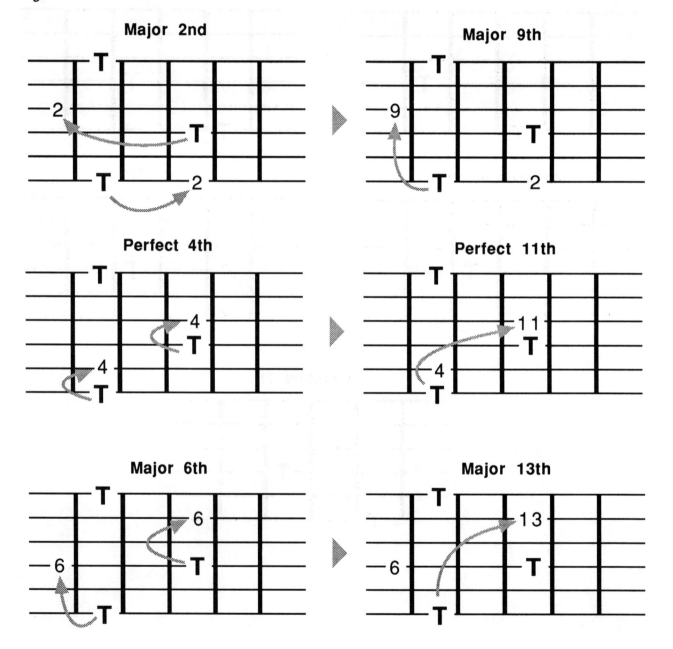

When assembling chords, it is not necessary to position each chord tone in its theoretically founded order, especially on the guitar, where the number of strings and their tuning confines, or limits, both the number of chord tones and chord voicings one can play. In other words, a chord played on the guitar may have its chord content voiced, or arranged, in many different ways. Specifically, upper chord extensions of 9ths, 11ths and 13ths may sometimes be voiced in the midst of a chord's foundational triad (e.g. R 3 5) or 7th chord (i.e. a triad with an added 7th scale degree); though your ear may occasionally tell you otherwise since these tones are most comfortable in a chord's upper most voices, the intermingling of chord tones is at times a more musical or at least practical choice, especially for guitarists. Hence, even when building different chord forms and voicings on the fingerboard, *thinking* of upper chord extensions in terms of their primary octave counter-parts in the midst of a chord's foundational triad or 7th chord is much more practical, and a faster means to an end (i.e. a faster and easier way of finding the optimal chord and voicing you desire), though these tones may ultimately be voiced anywhere in the chord.

When performing arpeggios in a musical context however, the voicing, or arrangement, of tones is more critical, since an arpeggios' identity relies more heavily upon the order in which its tones are heard; yet, thinking of upper chord extensions in terms of their primary octave counter-parts is still more advantageous.

This will be better understood in the next two chapters.

Here are a few of the more common of these larger intervallic patterns you may need to be familiar with.

Figure 4-34

minor 9th

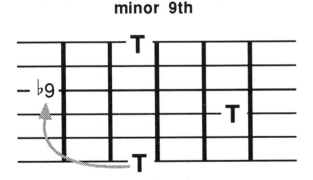

Augmented 9th

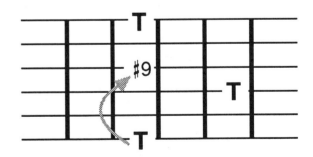

Augmented 11th

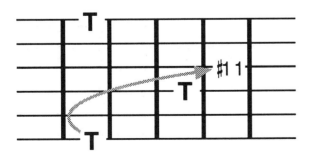

minor 13th

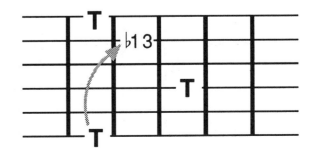

TEST YOURSELF
CHAPTER 4

1. Beginning with D# on the first fret of the fourth string find all unison tones on other strings.

2. Beginning with C# on the second fret of the second string find all the unison tones .

3. The diagrams below represent a tone on the guitar fingerboard.

   a) Indicate where a tone may be played one octave above the tone shown in the diagram.

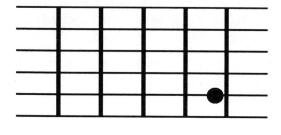 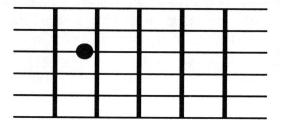

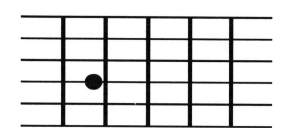 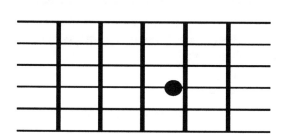

b) Indicate where a tone may be played one octave below the tone shown in the diagram.

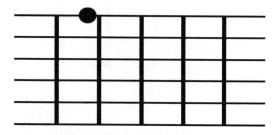 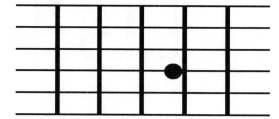

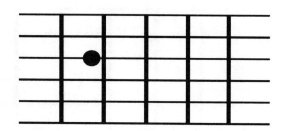 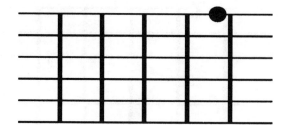

c) Indicate where every possible tone with the same letter-name may be found on the fingerboard. (These tones may be one or more octaves apart.)

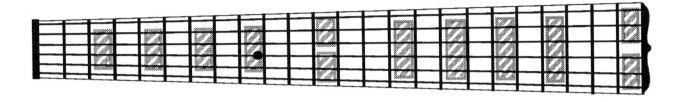

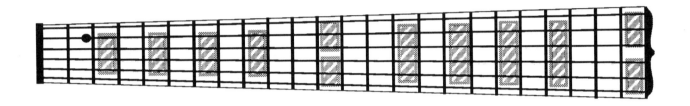

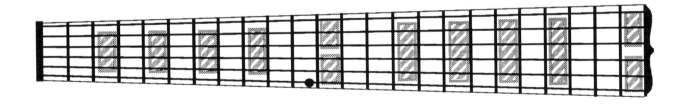

4. In the diagrams below, begin with the tonic and fill in all major scale tones.

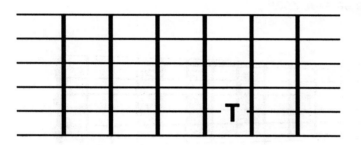

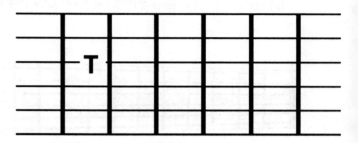

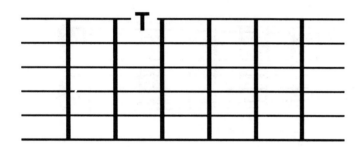

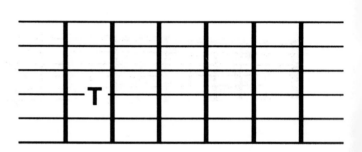

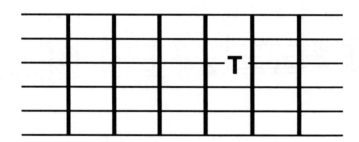

5. Identify the following intervallic fingerboard patterns.

a.

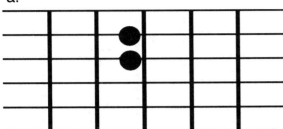

b.

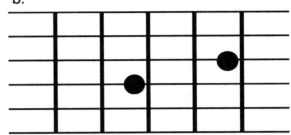

c.

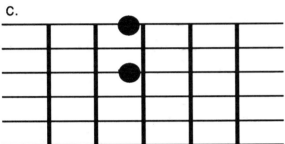

d.

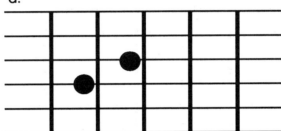

e.

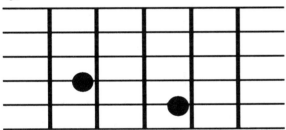

f.

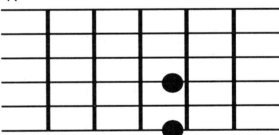

g.

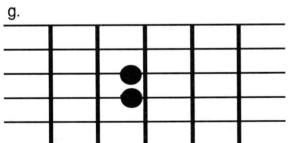

h.

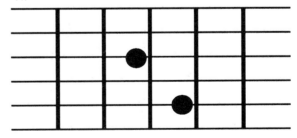

5.   (continued)

i.

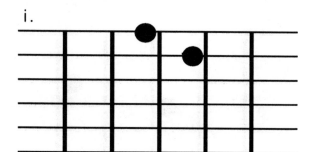

j.

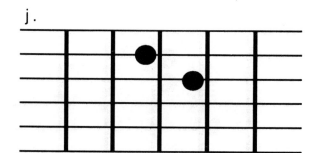

k.

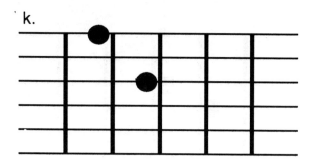

l.

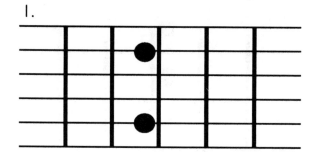

m.

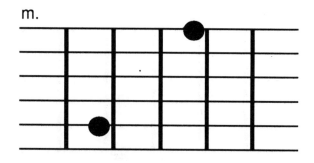

n

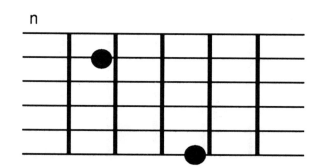

o.

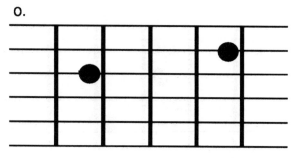

p.

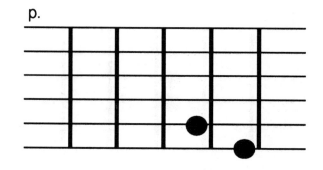

q.

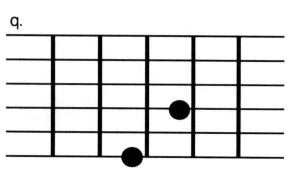

r.

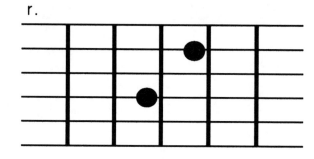

ANSWERS
TEST YOURSELF
CHAPTER 4

1.

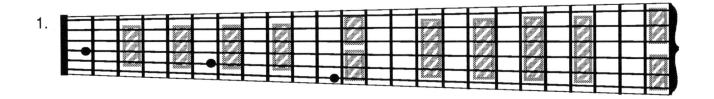

2.

3a.

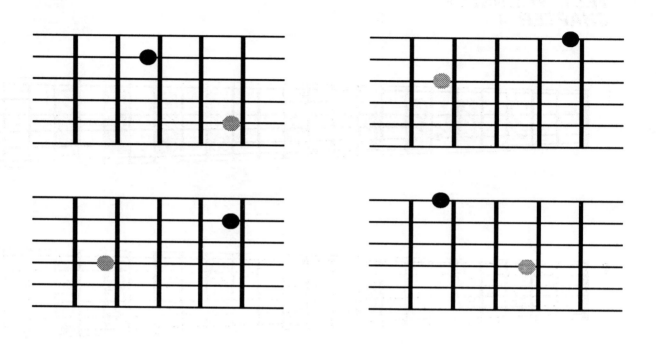

3b.

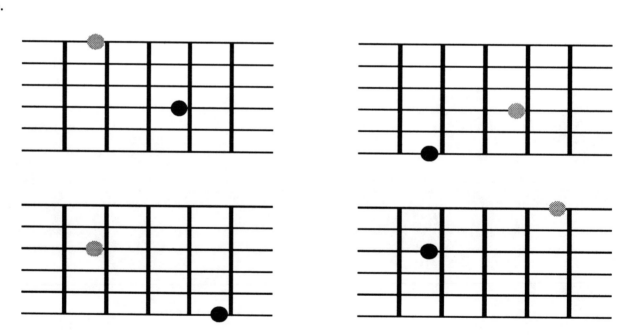

3c.

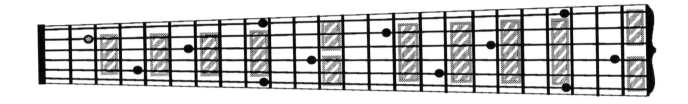

4.

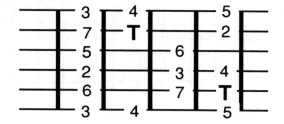 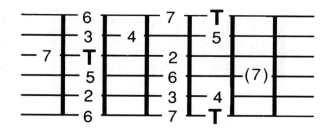

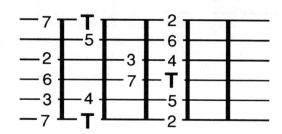 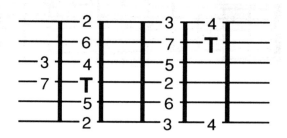

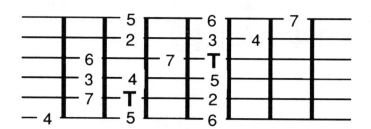

5.

a. Major 3	b. Perfect 5	i. Major 3	j. minor 3
c. Major 6	d. diminished 5 (or Augmented 4th)	k. minor 6 (or Augmented 5th)	l. Major 9
e. minor 3	f. minor 7	m. Major 13	n. Major 11
g. Perfect 4	h. Major 6 (or diminished 7)	o. Perfect 5	p. Major 3
		q. Major 7	r. minor 7

CHAPTER 5
CHORD ARPEGGIOS

As stated previously, a chord consists of three or more tones sounding simultaneously. An arpeggio, however, is the sounding of these chord tones consecutively, one after the other (or randomly). Knowing chord arpeggios thoroughly can radically improve a guitarist's ability to both assemble chords on the fingerboard as well as improvise melodically and harmonically with greater resourcefulness and prowess.

Like other guitar patterns, the best way to learn chord arpeggio patterns is within the framework of the basic octave patterns shown in Chapter 4.

The easiest example to begin with is the Major 7 chord (R 3 5 7) since it is contained entirely within the major scale. This arpeggio is shown in the first octave of Octave Region 1.

Figure 5-1

Octave Region 1

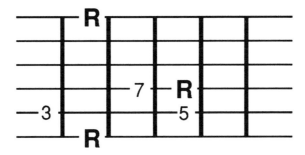

Now let's continue this arpeggio through the next octave of Octave Region 1.

Figure 5-2

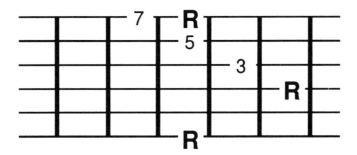

Here's what the Major 7 chord arpeggio looks like through two octaves in the first octave region.

Figure 5-3

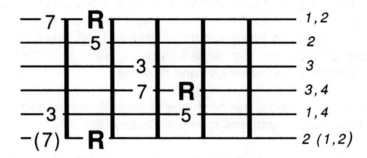

Remember, we are building Major 7 chord arpeggios. As with major scales, *a chord arpeggio's letter-name depends on the letter name of the root.*

Now let's build this major 7 arpeggio through the four remaining octave regions.

Figure 5-4

Octave Region 2

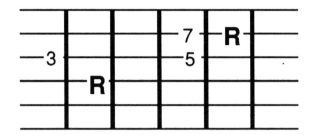

...extending upward

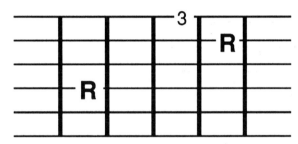

...extending downward

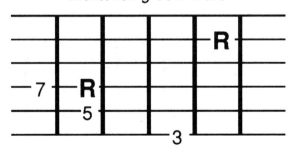

...all together

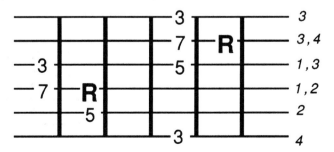

Figure 5-5

Octave Region 3

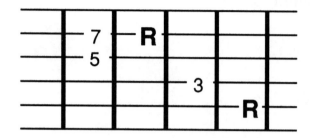

...extending upward

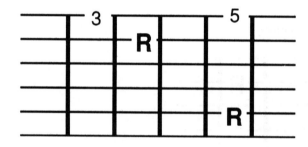

...extending downward

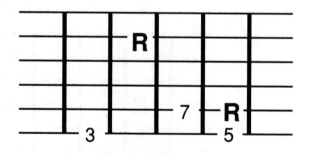

...all together

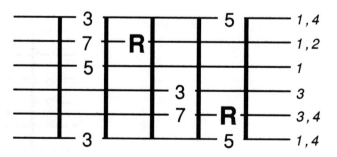

Figure 5-6

Octave Region 4

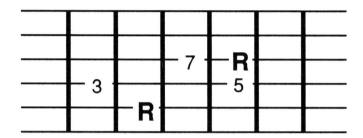

...extending upward

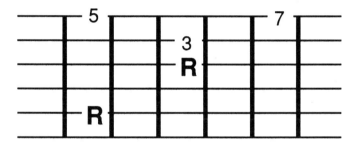

...extending downward

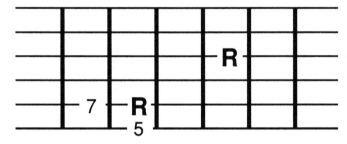

...all together

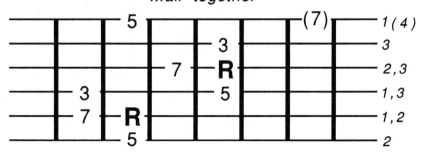

Figure 5-7

Octave Region 5

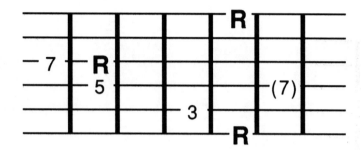

...extending upward

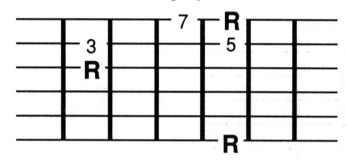

...extending downward

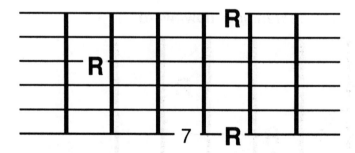

...all together

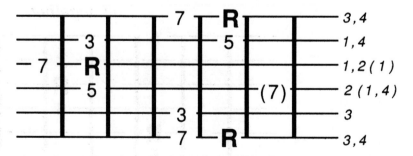

Now let's look at this chord arpeggio as it overlaps in all five octave regions. Remember, as with major scales, *any chord arpeggio overlaps with the same type chord arpeggio in either adjacent octave region.*

Figure 5-8

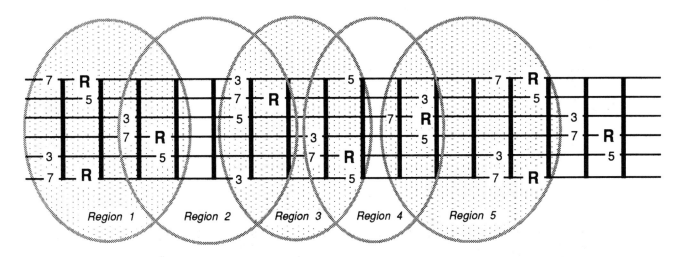

Do you remember what happened when we vertically transposed the major scale pattern in the first octave region in Figure 4-26? Observe the same result in Figure 5-9 as we vertically transpose the arpeggio pattern from the first octave region.

Figure 5-9

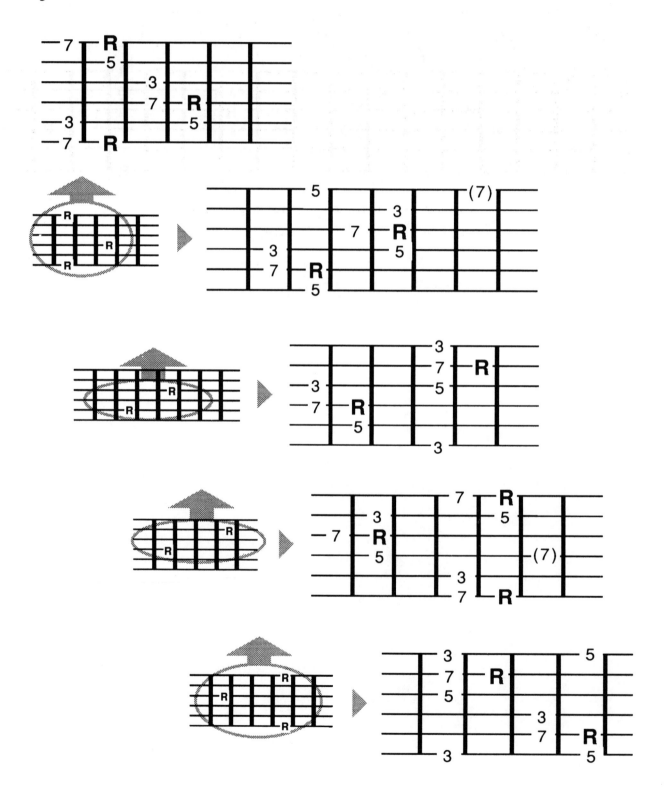

To continue, by learning arpeggios in terms of their individual interval components, constructing any other arpeggio is much easier. For example, since we know a Major 7 chord arpeggio is constructed R 3 5 7 and a "dominant" 7 chord arpeggio is constructed R 3 5 ♭7 , the only change necessary is lowering the 7th scale degree a half step in each Major 7 arpeggio pattern, altering an already learned pattern instead of trying to learn an entirely new pattern. In order to facilitate easier fingering, however, observe how chord arpeggio patterns may be modified slightly.

Figure 5-10

Octave Region 1

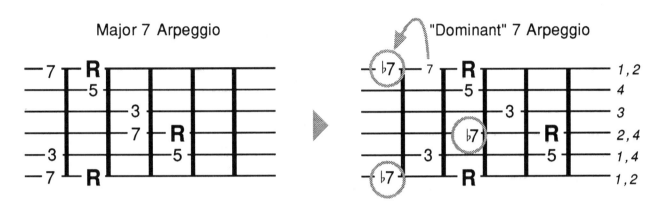

Major 7 Arpeggio   "Dominant" 7 Arpeggio

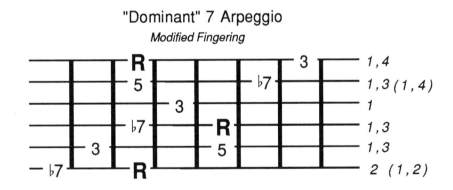

"Dominant" 7 Arpeggio
Modified Fingering

Figure 5-11

Octave Region 2

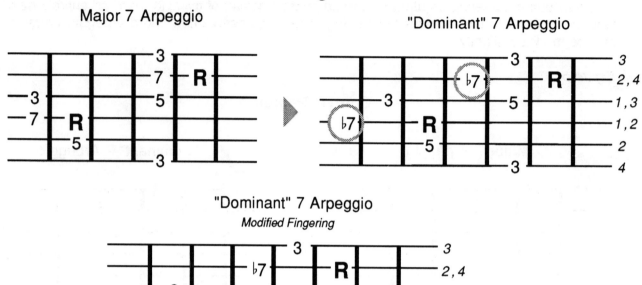

Major 7 Arpeggio

"Dominant" 7 Arpeggio

"Dominant" 7 Arpeggio
Modified Fingering

Figure 5-12

Octave Region 3

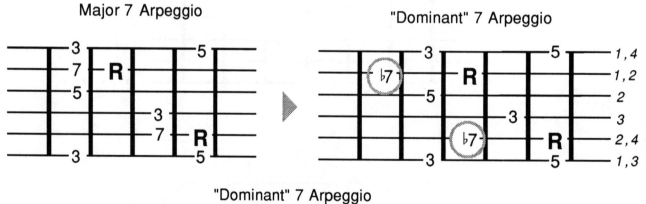

Major 7 Arpeggio

"Dominant" 7 Arpeggio

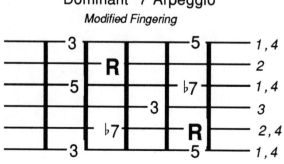

"Dominant" 7 Arpeggio
Modified Fingering

Figure 5-13

Octave Region 4

Major 7 Arpeggio

"Dominant" 7 Arpeggio

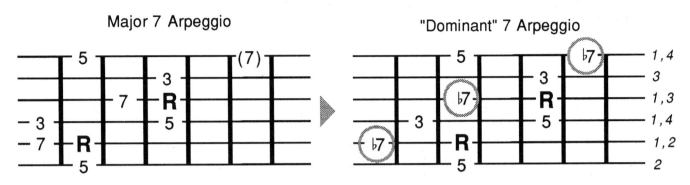

"Dominant" 7 Arpeggio
Modified Fingering

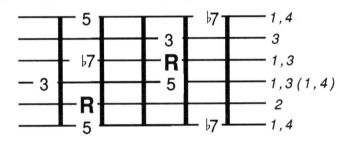

Figure 5-14

Octave Region 5

Major 7 Arpeggio

"Dominant" 7 Arpeggio

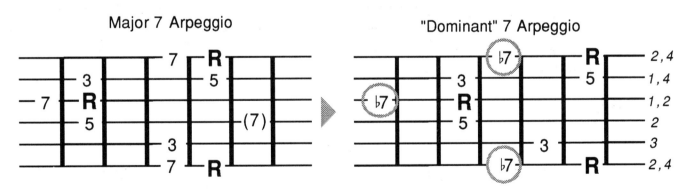

"Dominant" 7 Arpeggio
Modified Fingering

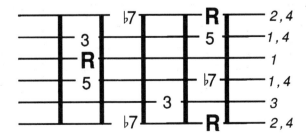

The minor 7 chord arpeggio (R ♭3 5 ♭7) is another important one to know. The diagrams to come show the minor 7 chord arpeggio patterns derived from the previously developed "dominant" 7 arpeggio patterns already containing the ♭7.

(Not wanting to be too repetitious, the author has omitted the middle step used in the previous diagrams.)

Figure 5-15

Octave Region 1

"Dominant" 7 Arpeggio   minor 7 Arpeggio
                                                   Modified fingering

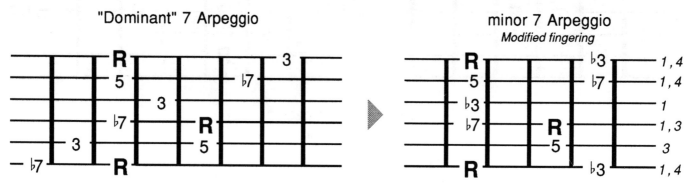

Figure 5-16

Octave Region 2

"Dominant" 7 Arpeggio   minor 7 Arpeggio
                                                   Modified Fingering

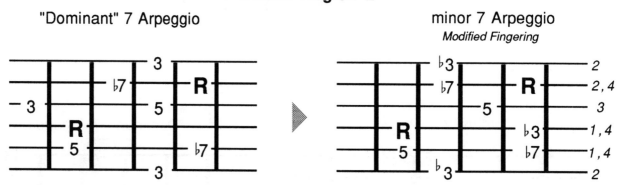

Figure 5-17

Octave Region 3

"Dominant" 7 Arpeggio   minor 7 Arpeggio
                                                   Modified Fingering

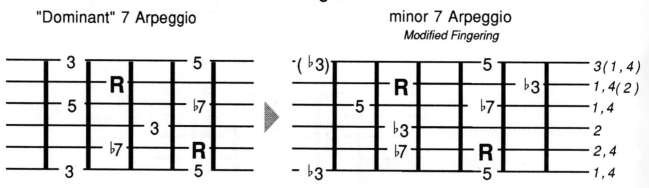

Figure 5-18

Octave Region 4

"Dominant" 7 Arpeggio

minor 7 Arpeggio
Modified Fingering

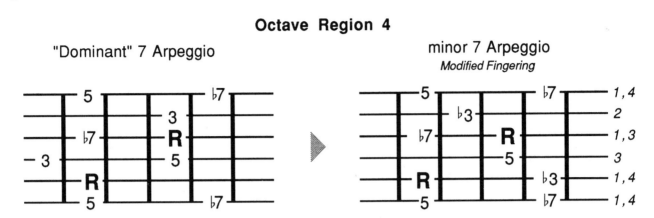

Figure 5-19

Octave Region 5

"Dominant" 7 Arpeggio

minor 7 Arpeggio
Modified Fingering

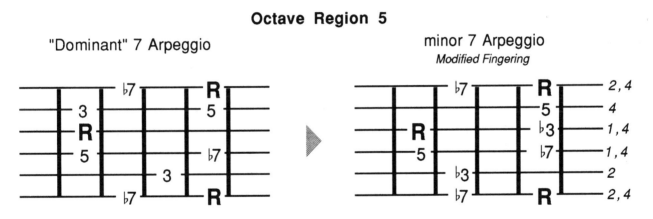

To conclude this chapter, let's look at some examples of larger arpeggio patterns for chords that extend beyond a single octave range. (Refer back to the text box on page 71.)

Figure 5-20

Major 13
Chord Arpeggio

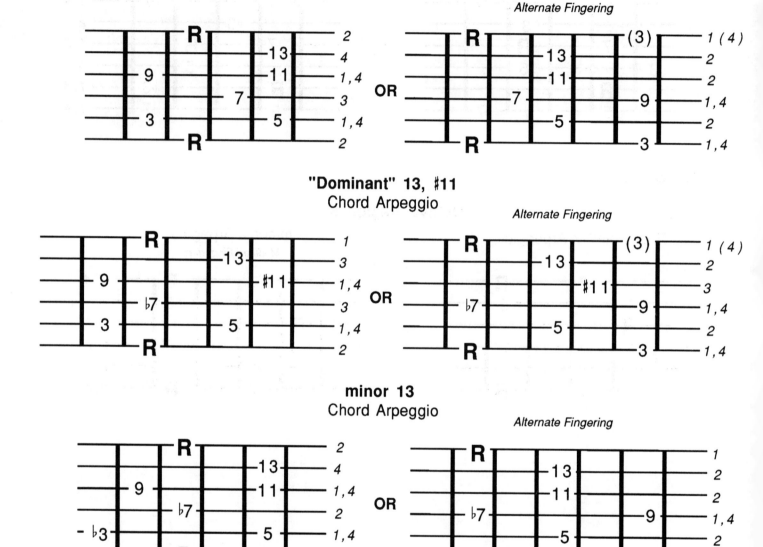

"Dominant" 13, #11
Chord Arpeggio

minor 13
Chord Arpeggio

Some other chord arpeggios are shown in detail in appendix four primarily for the purpose of showing how minute changes are made from one arpeggio pattern to another to facilitate easier fingering. By applying all the information from previous chapters up to this point, you should be able to construct any chord arpeggio anywhere on the fingerboard!

TEST YOURSELF
CHAPTER 5

1. Identify the chord tones by their intervallic number in these diagrams and name the chord arpeggio type (e.g. −7, ∘7, etc.) using the blank diagrams on the next page.

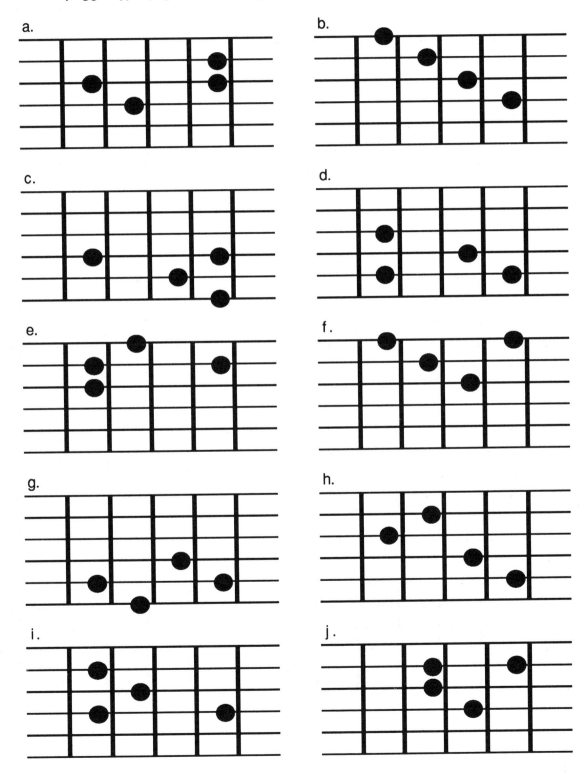

a.

b.

c.

d.

e.

f.

g.

h.

i.

j.

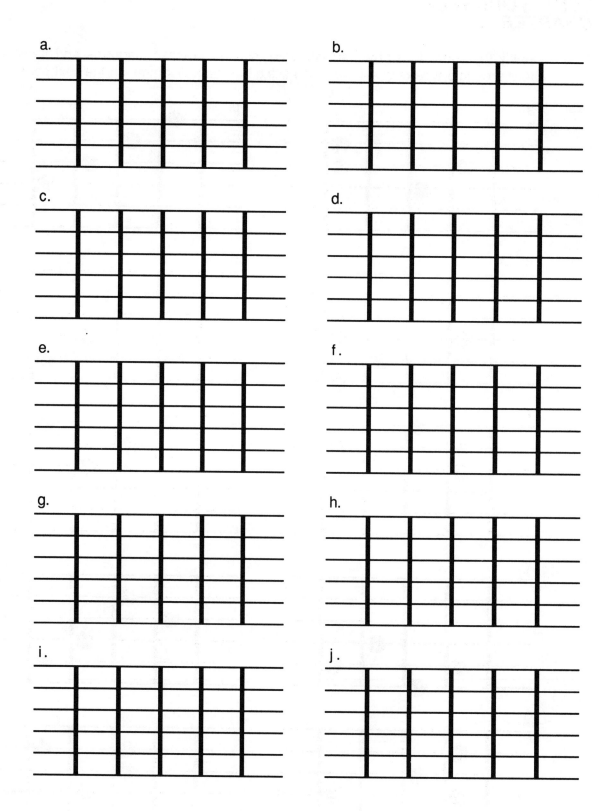

Chord Arpeggios

2. Follow the same directions in question 1 keeping in mind the arpeggios in this next exercise are not necessarily in root position.

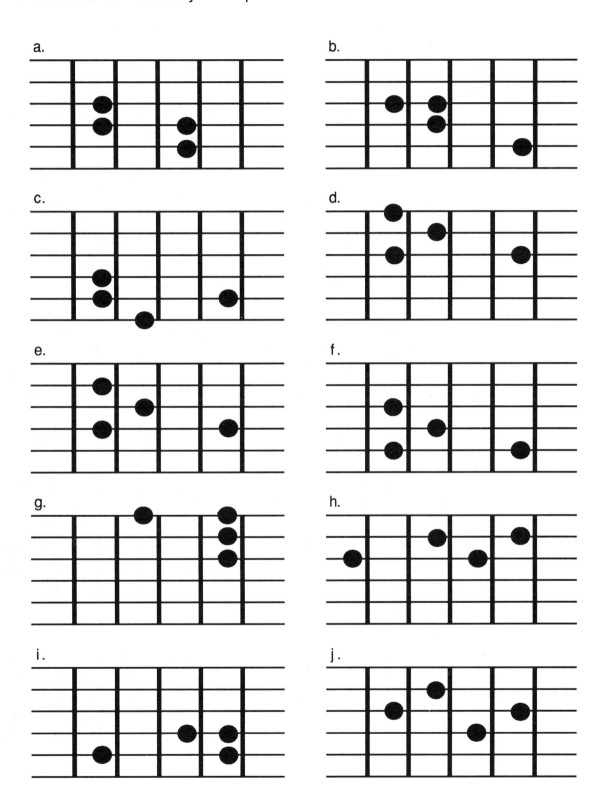

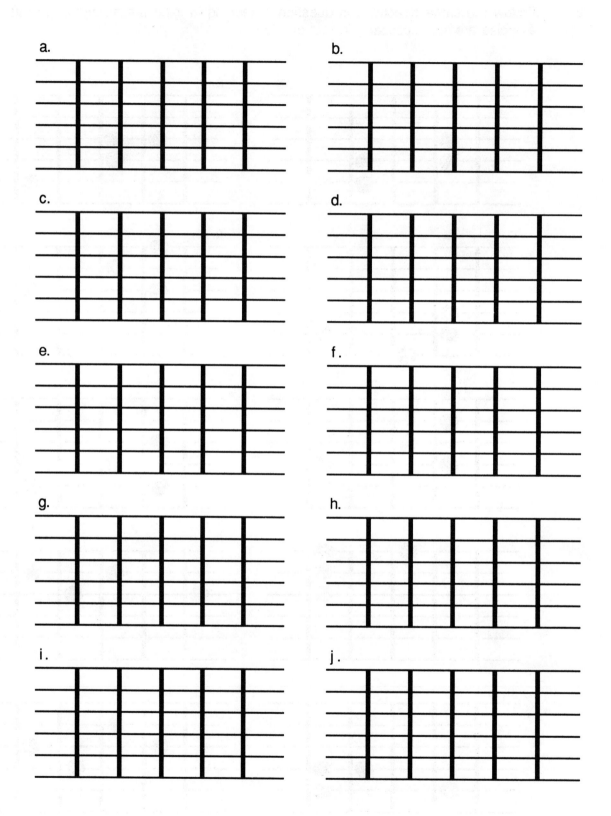

3. Fill in the remaining chord tones for the arpeggio patterns in each of the following diagrams beginning with the root.

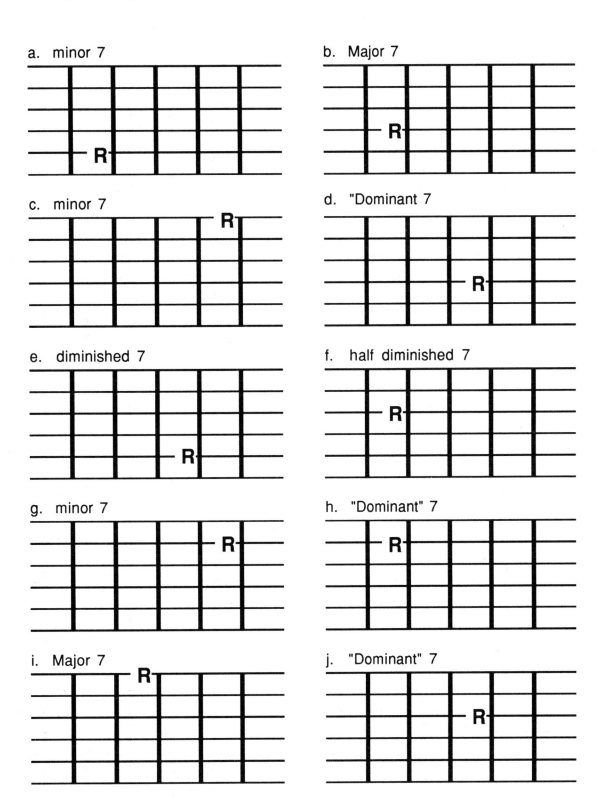

a. minor 7

b. Major 7

c. minor 7

d. "Dominant 7

e. diminished 7

f. half diminished 7

g. minor 7

h. "Dominant" 7

i. Major 7

j. "Dominant" 7

ANSWERS
SELF TEST
CHAPTER 5

1.

a. Major 7

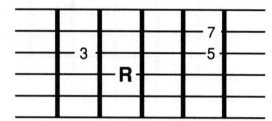

b. Major 7

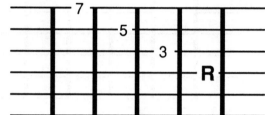

c. "Dominant" 7

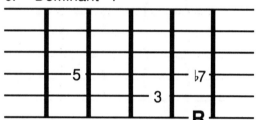

d. minor 7

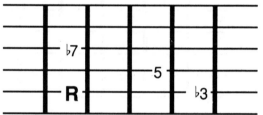

e. "Dominant" 7

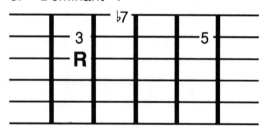

f. minor 7

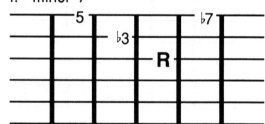

g. Major 7

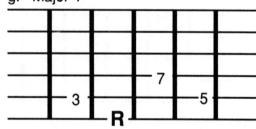

h. Major

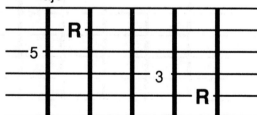

i. diminished 7

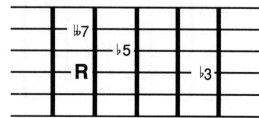

j. Augmented 7

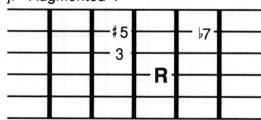

100   *Chord Arpeggios*

2.

a. minor 7

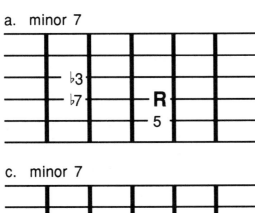

b. Major 7

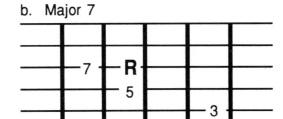

c. minor 7

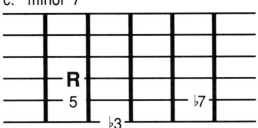

d. "Dominant 7

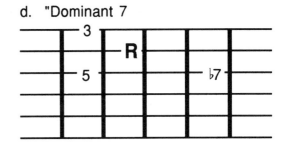

e. diminished 7

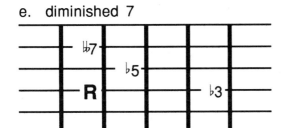

f. half diminished 7

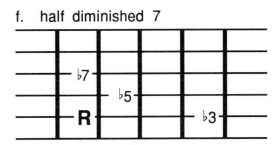

g. minor 7

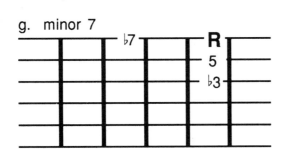

h. "Dominant" 7

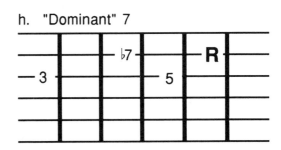

i. Major 7

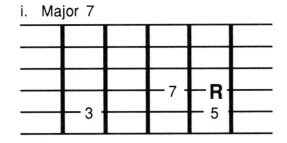

j. "Dominant" 7

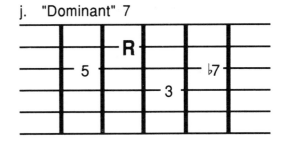

3.

a. minor 7
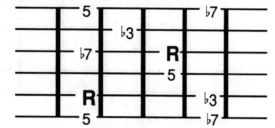

b. Major 7
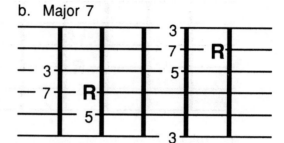

c. minor 7
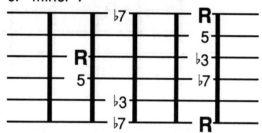

d. "Dominant 7
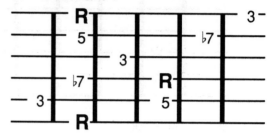

e. diminished 7
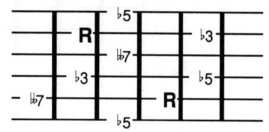

f. half diminished 7
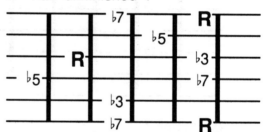

g. minor 7
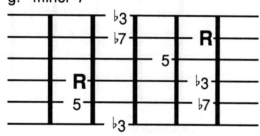

h. "Dominant" 7
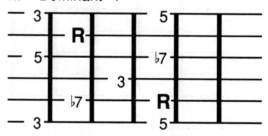

i. Major 7
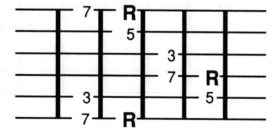

j. "Dominant" 7
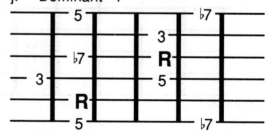

CHAPTER 6
GUITAR CHORDS

For the major scale and chord arpeggios the term "pattern" is used to describe a fixed arrangement of tones played *sequentially* (or possibly randomly) on the fingerboard. For chords, the term "form" is used to describe a fixed arrangement of tones played *simultaneously* on the fingerboard that may be treated in the same manner as scale or arpeggio patterns in terms of how they transpose across or along the fingerboard.

To begin, let's take a chord most everyone is familiar with C major.

Figure 6-1

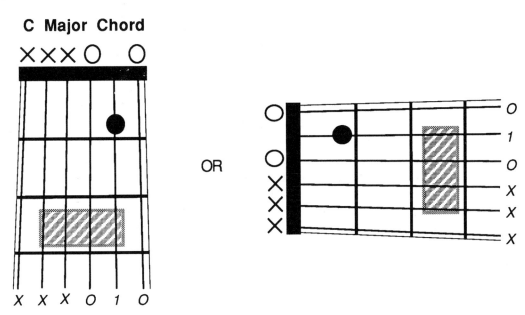

C Major Chord

OR

But instead of looking at this chord the way many are accustomed as in Figure 6-1, let's look at it a different way, as a major chord form.

Figure 6-2

Major Chord Form

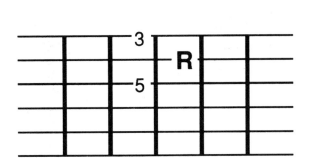

As with major scale and arpeggio patterns, *the letter name of the chord form depends upon the letter-name of the root.* So, if we position this chord form so that the root on the 2nd string is at the 1st fret, then we will have a C major chord because the tone at the 1st fret of the 2nd string is C.

Moving this chord form horizontally along the strings enables us to play all possible major chord names.

Figure 6-3

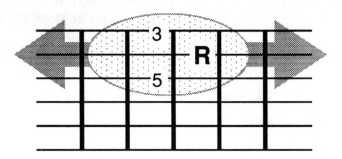

If we want to play a C# major chord, for example, all we need to do is move this entire chord form up one half step so that the root of the chord form is C#. When playing a C major chord using this form, there are two strings that were played open (without any fingers on the fingerboard). When we move this chord form up a half step, in order to maintain the integrity of the major chord form (keeping every part of the form [every tone] in unchanging relation to each other), those tones played as open strings will have to move up a half step with every other part of the form. In other words, you will have to rearrange your fingering in order to play (finger) those two tones on the 1st and 3rd strings that were previously open (un-fingered). This principle holds true for *all* chord forms containing open strings!

Figure 6-4

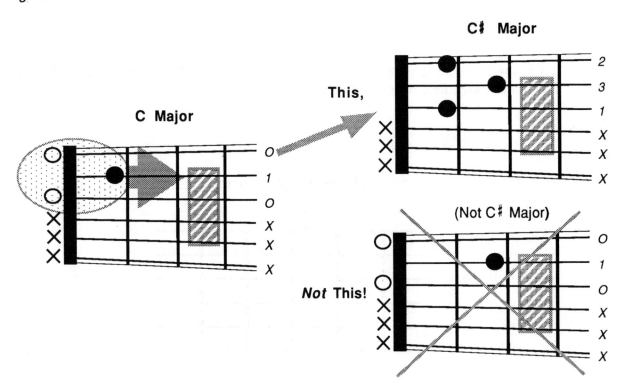

Now let's try transposing this chord form vertically across the strings.

Figure 6-5

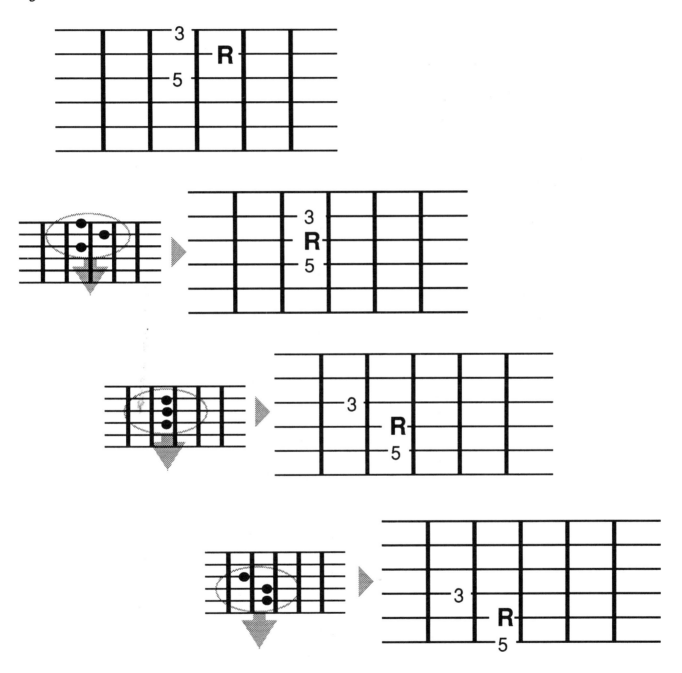

The example in Figure 6-5 illustrates how different chord forms with an identical voicing (i.e. intervallic arrangement of tones) are generated from one single chord form. Transposing chords vertically is a great way to create different chord forms with an identical or similar voicing.

Now let's expand our original chord form by applying some principles we've already learned. First, remember a major chord must contain its essential elements, R 3 5, in order to be a major chord.

Second, applying our knowledge of octave patterns, additional chord tones may be added an octave (or multiple octaves) apart from each original chord tone thus creating entirely new chord forms.

Figure 6-6

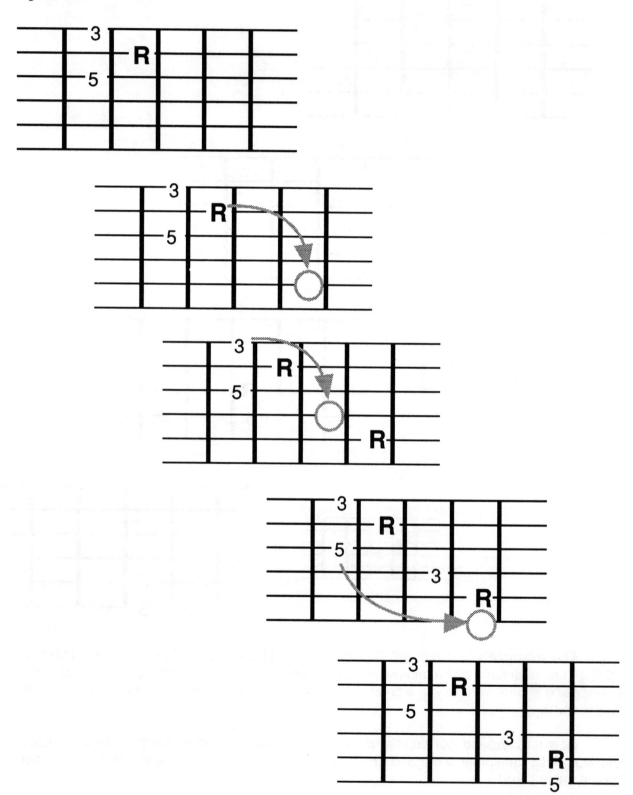

There are several items to notice here:

1)   The original major triad is duplicated an octave lower in a slightly different form while maintaining the exact same voicing (intervallic arrangement of tones).

Figure 6-7

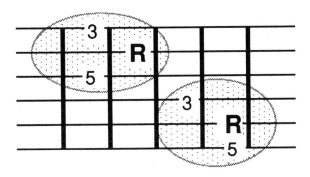

2)   The lowest sounding chord tone may be changed to create different inversions:

Figure 6-8

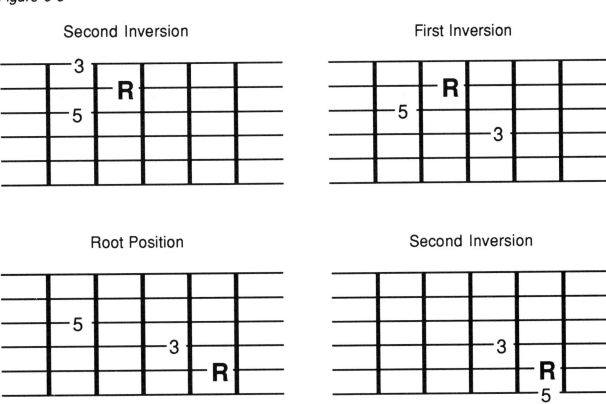

Second Inversion   First Inversion

Root Position   Second Inversion

Remember, *a chord's root position or inversion is determined only by the chord's lowest sounding tone, no matter how the remainder of the chord is voiced or whether any other chord tones occur more than once.* For example, these are all first inversion major chords (or Major chord forms):

Figure 6-9

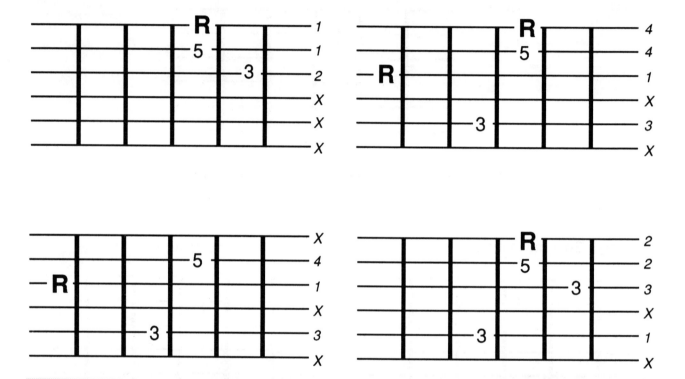

3)   This procedure may be continued across the entire fingerboard in a similar manner: a) either changing the octave of one or more tones; b) duplicating one or more tones; or c) removing duplicate chord tones. This is one way of creating a variety of chord voicings or different chord forms altogether. However, always be careful to include all characteristic chord tones (R 3 5 in this example). Here are some other possible voicings and forms developed by the same procedure:

Figure 6-10

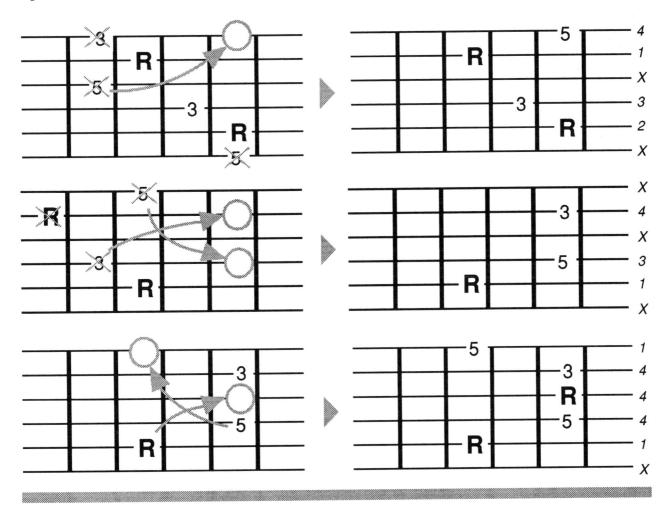

Note:

    This next chord is vague without a 3rd, and is not a major chord, though it may pass as major or minor because of its ambiguity.

Figure 6-11

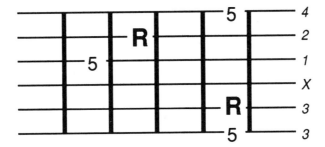

This next voicing may pass as a major chord even though it lacks a 5th, since 5ths do least to contribute to a chord's character:

Figure 6-12

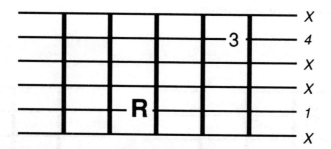

4)   A comprehensive "map" of all the tones in a Major chord may be generated in a like manner, that is, by continually duplicating chord tones an octave, and multiple octaves, apart from each original chord tone, traversing the entire fingerboard. In other words, assemble Major chord arpeggios in all five octave regions as in the previous chapter! [1]

Figure 6-13

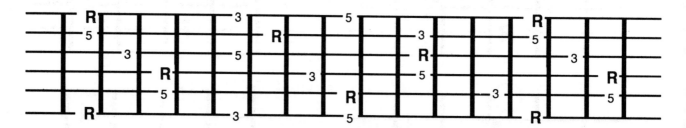

Do you see any major chord forms "hidden" in Figure 6-13? By simply selecting at least one of each essential chord tone in any location on the fingerboard, an enormous number of different chord forms and voicings may be created. Of course, you should select chord tones that are physically possible to play, either with your fingerboard hand, or as open strings, or a combination of the two. Let's find a few in just the first octave region.

Figure 6-14

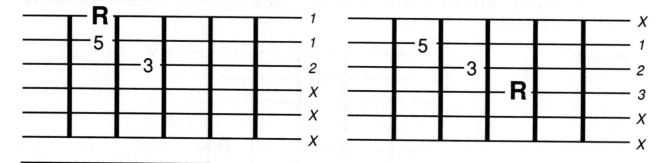

[1]   Don't forget, the letter-name of the root is the letter-name of the chord!

Figure 6-14 (cont'd)

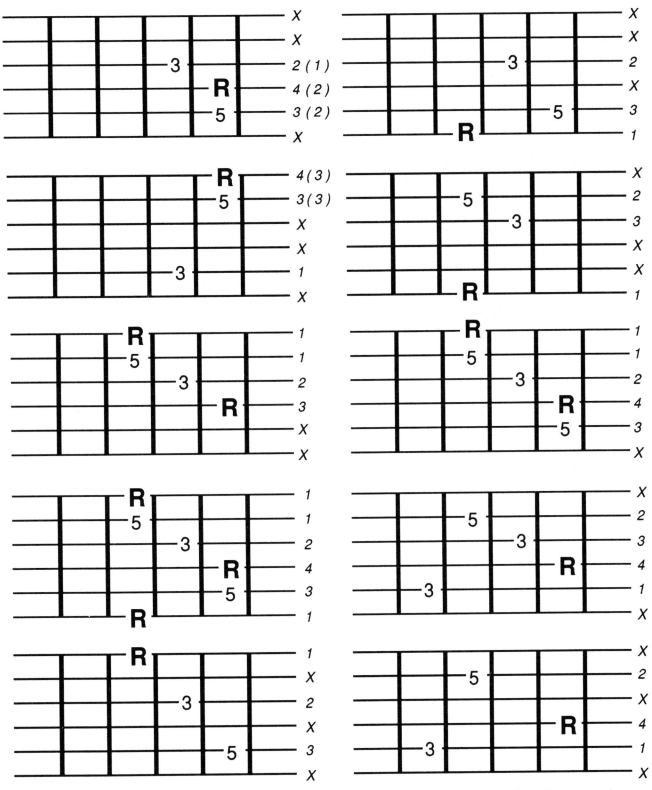

Having a firm grasp of essential fingerboard patterns, chord construction theory and chord arpeggios provides the guitarist with an orderly, sensible means of constructing vast amounts of chord forms and voicings.

A few words about **chord voicing**. . .

A chord's voicing may vary from having the closest possible intervals from tone to tone (3rds or 2nds), to farther spread, more open, intervals of a 5th or greater from tone to tone. For example, the chords in Figure 6-15 have no interval greater than a 3rd between voices and are considered as having "close", or "closed", voicings.

Figure 6-15

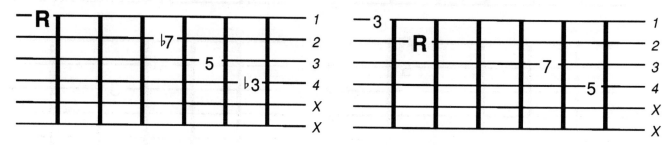

On the other hand, the chords in Figure 6-16 have a greater span between intervals and are considered as having more "spread", or "open", voicings.

Figure 6-16

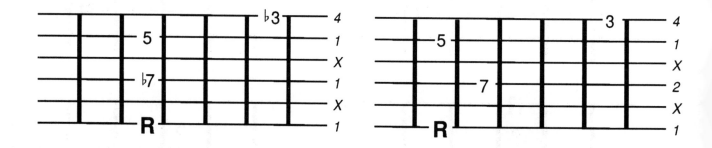

Other ways of controlling a chord's voicing is by:

1)   Choosing specific chord tones as:
         a) the highest sounding voice; or,
         b) lowest sounding voice (i.e. choosing the chord's root position or other possible inversion); or,
         c) middle sounding voices; or,
         d) all of the above; then,

2)   by making a voice or voices of one chord melodically lead to a voice or voices of a succeeding chord; and/or,

3)   by using carefully chosen chord textures, or densities, varying from "thin" to "thick".

Figure 6-17

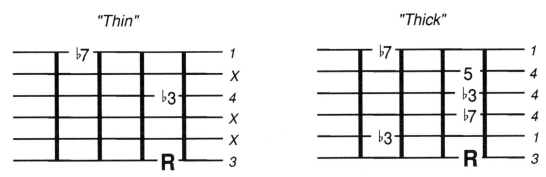

One chord voicing is perhaps more appropriate than another depending upon the musical situation. Using carefully chosen chord voicing and voice leading from chord to chord, not just "swatting" the first chord that comes to mind, enables the *musician* to create meaningful melodic harmonies and effectively communicate musical ideas.

Another important aspect of chord voicing is the relationship between a chord's intervallic structure (i.e. the distance from tone to tone within the chord voicing) and its pitch. Specifically, the resonant quality of a chord voicing with respect to its intervallic structure is directly proportional to the height or depth of its pitch; that is, a chord voicing with smaller and/or more dissonant intervals sounds more resonant, or clear, as it ascends in pitch, and sounds increasingly less resonant, or muddy, as it descends in pitch. Consequently, larger and/or more consonant intervals within a chord voicing retain their clarity (i.e. resist the tendency to become muddy) at lower depths in pitch. Try experimenting with any of the above chord forms to test this phenomenon.

Let's try working through another example using a common chord many beginning guitar students are familiar with: A minor 7.

Figure 6-18

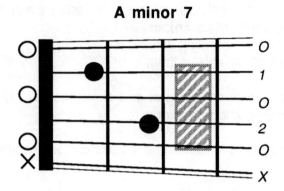

A minor 7

First, let's use some common sense to unveil the intervallic content of this chord form. Since we call this chord A minor 7, "A", as you've learned by now, is the root chord tone:
1) Where is "A" located in this area of the fingerboard?

Figure 6-19

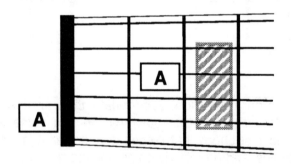

Figure 6-20

2) Build an A minor 7 chord arpeggio in this same fingerboard region;

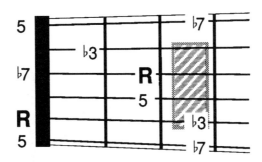

3) Thus, the intervallic content of the original chord form is contained within this chord arpeggio.

Figure 6-21

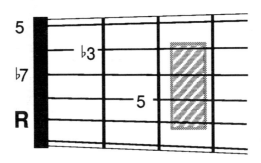

Naturally, this chord form may be transposed horizontally to perform any minor 7 chord.

Figure 6-22

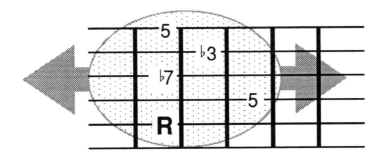

Remember, when transposing any chord form horizontally, all open strings must move as part of the form.

Figure 6-23

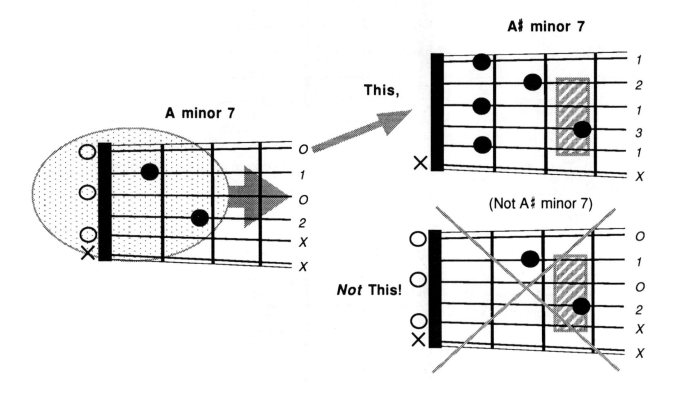

Transposing this form vertically creates other chord forms.

Figure 6-24

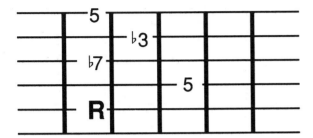

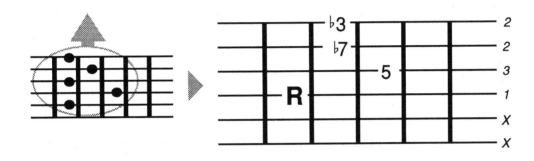

OR

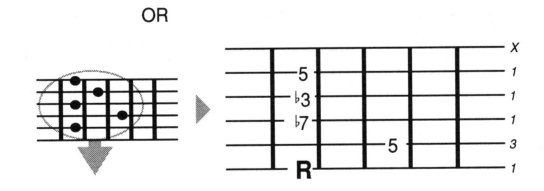

The next diagram shows the possibility of either changing the octave of one or more tones, duplicating one or more tones, or removing duplicate chord tones.

Figure 6-25

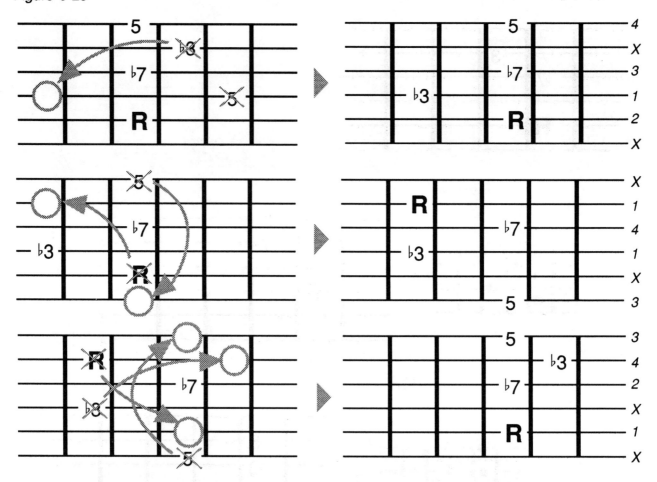

Finally, a chord arpeggio "map" traversing the entire fingerboard may be generated to reveal every possible chord form and voicing.

Figure 6-26

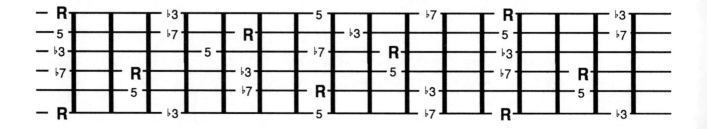

Now begin to assemble as many minor 7 chord forms as possible. Here are some chords you may find.

Figure 6-27

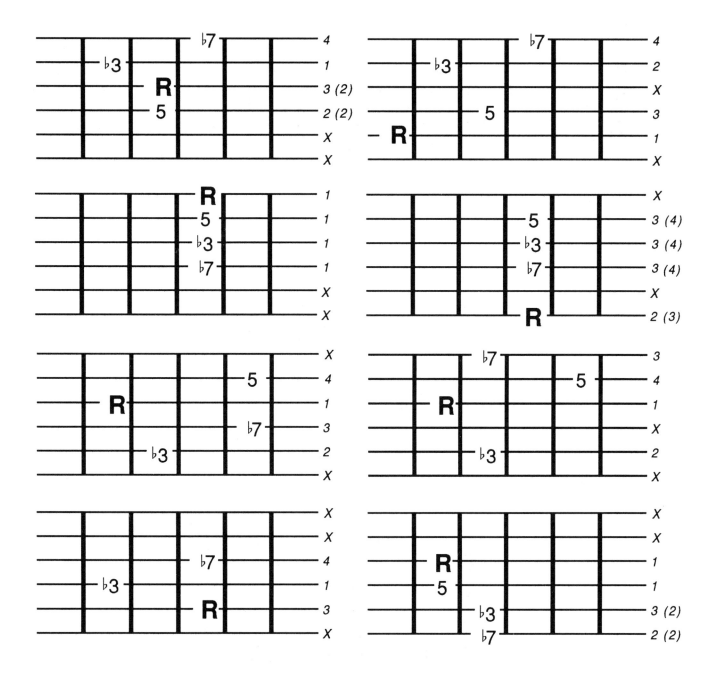

Next, try finding a more difficult chord, G+7($\flat$9), supposing we do not know any fingerboard forms for this chord at this point. All we do know is the chord content (from Chapter 3): R 3 $\sharp$5 $\flat$7 $\flat$9 . The first step might be to find every root ("G", in this case) on the entire fingerboard, or in a specific octave region.

Figure 6-28

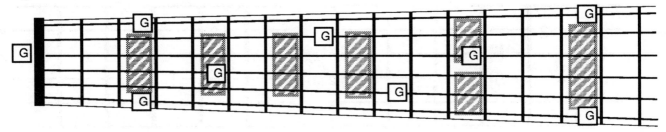

Next, we may assemble a G+7($\flat$9) chord arpeggio in any fingerboard region we choose (depending on our preference of voicing within a given harmonic context). For example...

Figure 6-29

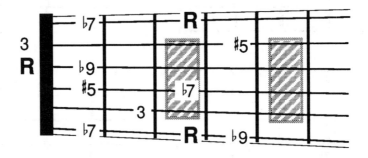

Thus, Figure 6-30 shows a possible chord we might extract from the previous arpeggio.

Figure 6-30

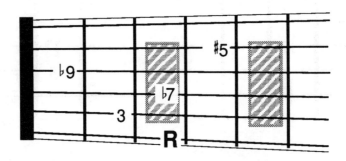

Chords with extensions beyond a 7th (9ths, 11ths, and 13ths) are best voiced with their extensions in the highest sounding voices of the chord, usually keeping the root, 3rd, 5th and/or 7th in the lower voices. There may be quite a few exceptions to this. Your ear is the final judge. (Refer back to the text box on page 71.)

Of course, this chord form may be transposed horizontally as well as vertically.

Figure 6-31

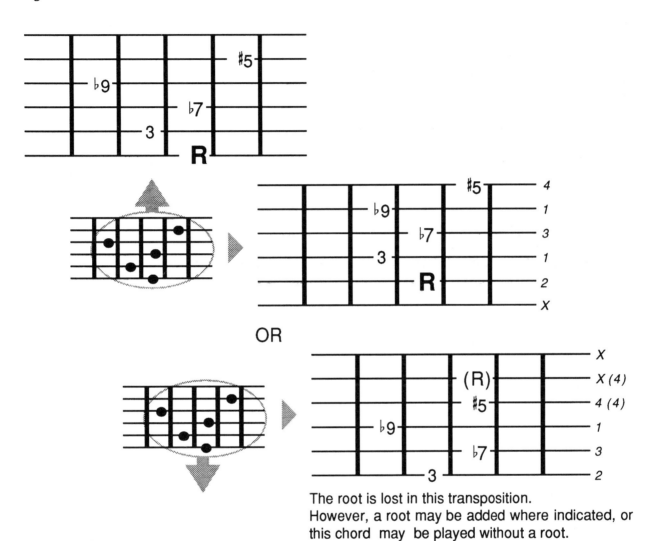

OR

The root is lost in this transposition.
However, a root may be added where indicated, or
this chord may be played without a root.

As you can see, the greater the number of chord tones, the more limited the vertical distance a chord form may move before more severe changes are made to maintain the integrity of the chord content, i.e. relocating chord tones lost in the transposition because of a limited number of guitar strings.

Though the omission of the root in Figure 6-31 is the result of the vertical transposition, guitarists often omit roots on chords with a 7th scale degree or greater either:

    a) when accompanied by a bass or other instrument likely to play the root or lowest chord tone;

    b) when desiring a particular voicing without a root, since the root is the least colorful tone to the 5th and consequently a likely choice for omission; or,

    c) when desiring a more economical or easier fingering.

In certain contexts, a guitarist may even omit a chord's root *and* 5th, leaving only the 3rd, 7th and any other upper extensions or altered tones as these are the most colorful and distinguishing chord tones. On the contrary, in other situations a guitarist may omit all tones except the root and 5th for a more open and vibrant sound. "Heavy Metal" guitarists refer to these as "power-chords" using them frequently in their music.

    Therefore, the guitarist who understands both his musical environment, and the essential fundamentals and creative possibilities of harmony, may feel free to omit a chord's root, 5th or any other tone in the quest for a particular musical color or texture, or for simply an easier fingering.

Next, this chord form may be manipulated tone by tone,...

Figure 6-32

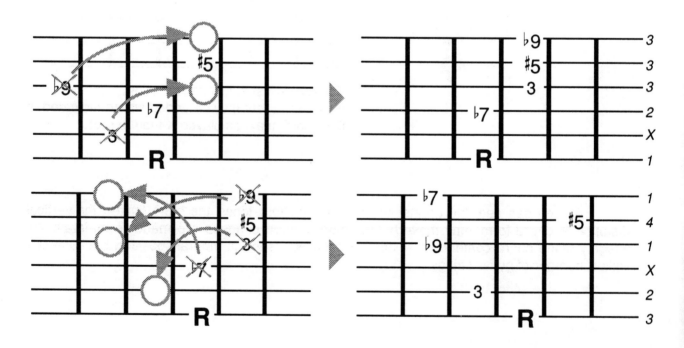

...or a chord arpeggio "map" may be generated revealing every possible chord form and voicing.

Figure 6-33

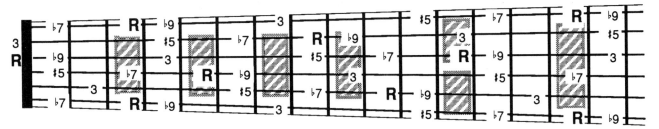

Then, from this map, a variety of specially voiced chord forms may be chosen.

Figure 6-34

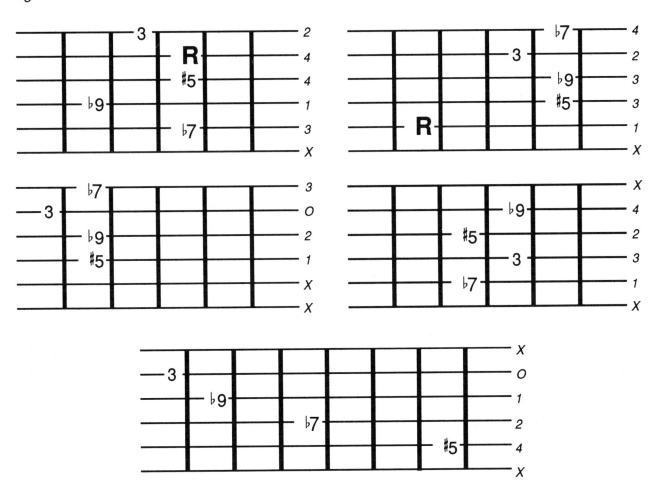

Of course, going through all these procedures may not be necessary to obtain a particular chord. The guitarist may approach a desired chord from a number of different directions to ultimately arrive at the desired result. The approach one takes depends upon how much information he has about the chord to begin with, and how he prefers to mold that chord to a particular musical situation.

String Groupings and Chord Form Families

Creating chord forms by the method demonstrated in this chapter introduces a myriad of, perhaps overwhelming, possibilities. To help narrow the field of choice when beginning to learn new chord forms, especially those with four tones or greater, choose chord forms adhering to a specific group of strings, namely, the groups of strings numbered: 4 3 2 1, 5 4 3 2, 6 5 4 3, 5 3 2 1, or, 6 4 3 2. The "dominant" 7 chords in Figure 6-36 are examples of some very useful chord forms making use of these string groupings. (All the chords in this diagram happen to be in root position, however chords are available in these string groupings in any inversion.)

Figure 6-35

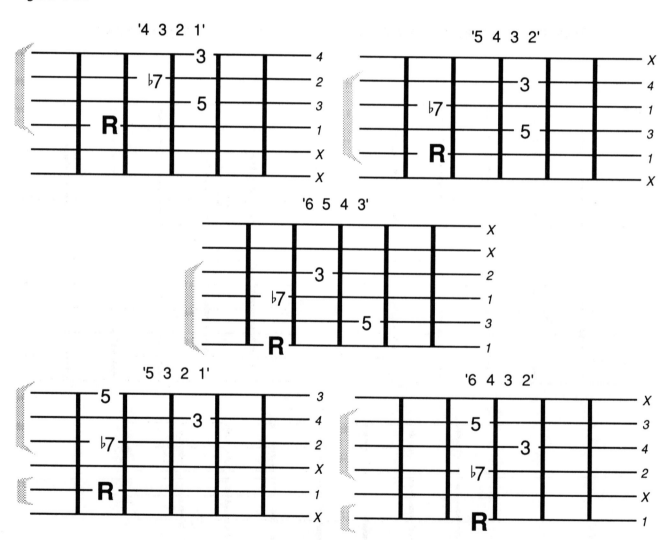

Chord forms occurring on these groups of strings are considered basic essentials by many, having proven themselves invaluable to guitarists past and present.

Furthermore, not only is selecting certain string groupings helpful in the chord learning process, recognizing *chord form families* related by either string grouping or root location (i.e. general fingerboard locale) is also very helpful. In Figure 6-36 for example, each *different* chord makes use of the *same* group of strings, and their is a variation of only one tone progressing from chord to chord. Hence, the following chord forms are very closely related and may be considered in the same chord form family.

Figure 6-36

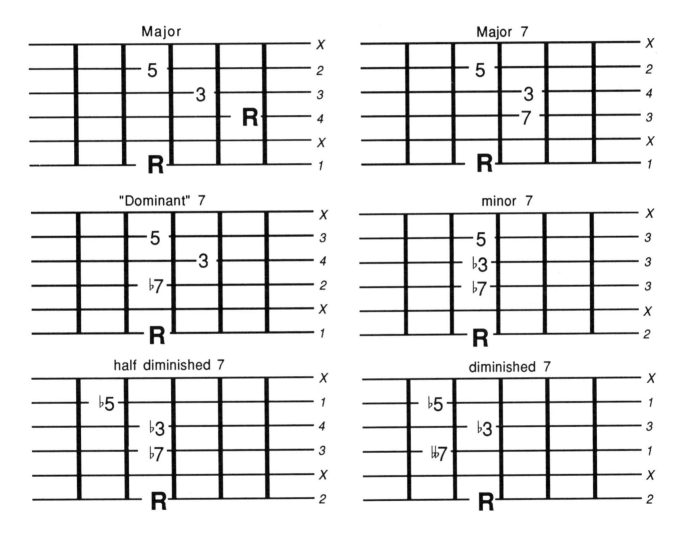

Learning and associating chords in this way is a great way to quickly increase your chord vocabulary.

Chord Plurality

Plurality is a term used to describe the containment of one or more smaller chords within a larger chord.

For example, compare the C Major and A minor 7 chords shown earlier in this chapter. Upon closer observation, notice the C Major chord is actually contained within the A minor 7 chord. Specifically, a minor 7 chord (e.g. A minor 7) always contains a major chord (e.g. C Major) whose root is the ♭3rd of the same (i.e. the root of the major chord is the ♭3rd of the minor 7 chord).

Figure 6-37

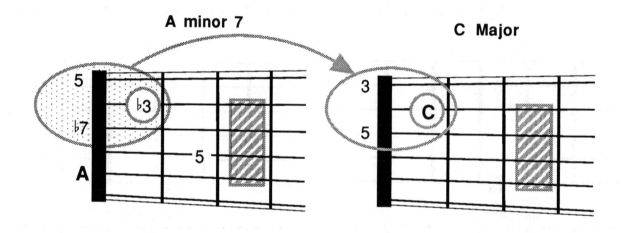

Likewise, this same peculiarity may be found observing a +7($\flat$9) chord (though a more mature understanding and comprehension of this book's content up to this point makes the forthcoming observation a little easier). For example, lets consider G^{+7}($\flat$9). In this case you'll find F$-$7($\flat$5) or F$\emptyset$7 contained within G^{+7}($\flat$9). Specifically, a +7($\flat$9) chord (e.g. G^{+7}($\flat$9)) always contains a half diminished 7 chord (e.g. F$\emptyset$7) whose root is the $\flat$7th of the same (i.e. the root of the $\emptyset$7 chord is the $\flat$7th of the +7($\flat$9) chord).

Figure 6-38

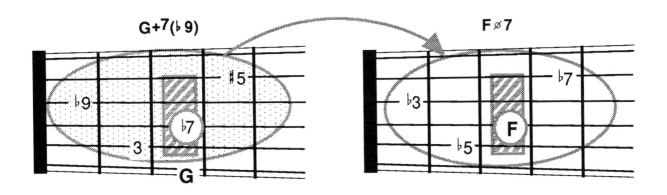

Taking this example a step further, a $\emptyset$7 chord (e.g. F$\emptyset$7) always contains a minor chord (e.g. A$\flat$ minor) whose root is the $\flat$3 of the same. (The F$\emptyset$7 chord is voiced differently in Figure 6-39 to illustrate this example more clearly.)

Figure 6-39

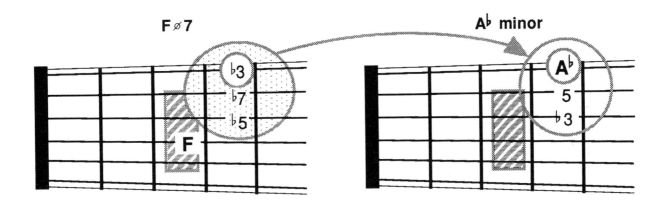

Here are some more examples of chord pluralities.

Figure 6-40

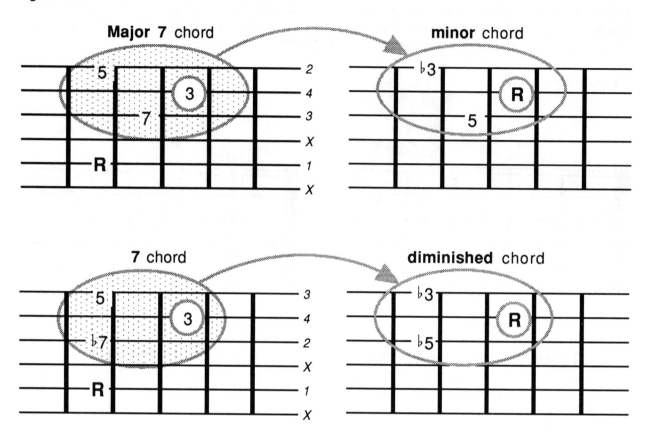

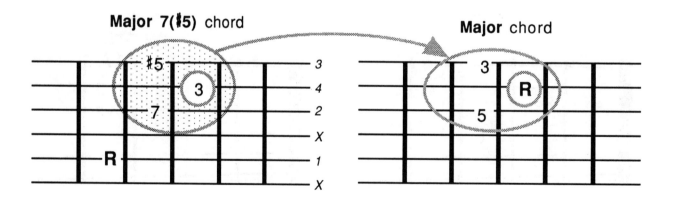

Understanding the plurality of chords is very useful when playing with a bassist or other instrument(s) likely to play chord roots. For example, playing smaller chord components of larger chords can help the guitarist add more variety and interest to his repertoire, or simply help him move more easily through fast chord changes.

Nine, eleven and thirteen chords have even more pluralities. Here are a few examples.

Figure 6-41

Larger Chord	This tone of the larger chord is the ROOT of the smaller chord(s)	Smaller Chords
Major 9	3	minor *or* minor 7
	5	Major
"Dominant" 9	3	diminished *or* half diminished 7
	5	minor
minor 9	♭3	Major *or* Major 7
	5	minor
Major 7(♯11)	3	minor *or* minor 7 *or* minor 9
	5	Major *or* Major 7
	7	minor
9 sus 4	5	minor *or* minor 7
	♭7	Major
9(♯11)	3	diminished *or* half diminished 7 *or* ∅7(9)
	5	minor *or* minor/Major 7
	♭7	augmented
	9	augmented
	♯11	augmented *or* augmented 7
minor 11	♭3	Major *or* Major 7 *or* Major 9
	5	minor *or* minor 7
	♭7	Major
Major 13 (♯11)	3	minor *or* minor 7 *or* minor 9 *or* minor 11
	5	Major *or* Major 7 *or* Major 9
	7	minor *or* minor 7
	9	Major
13 sus 4	5	minor *or* minor 7 *or* minor 9
	♭7	Major *or* Major 7
	9	minor

Augmented or diminished chords contained within larger chords have multiple plural possibilities.

For example, Any 7(♭9) chord without its root is a diminished 7 chord (○7). Consequently, because of the ○7 chord's unique nature, there are four different 7(♭9) chords containing the same ○7 chord; eg. C7(♭9), G♭7(♭9), A7(♭9), and E♭7(♭9) without their roots spell the same ○7 chord spelled: B♭ E G D♭.

Likewise, any minor/Major 7 chord without it's root is an augmented chord. Consequently, because of the augmented chord's unique nature, there are three different minor/Major 7 chords containing the same augmented chord; e.g. A minor/Major 7, C♯ minor/Major 7 and F minor/Major 7 without their roots spell the same augmented chord spelled: G♯ C E. (Also notice the 9(♯11) chord in Figure 6-41.)

Be sure to apply this concept of plurality to **arpeggios** as well as chords!

Tritone Chord Relationships

Every "dominant" 7 type chord has another closely related "dominant" 7 chord whose root is the interval of a diminished 5th or *tritone* apart. In the context of harmonic progression, chords with this relationship are considered *tritone*, or ♭*5*, *substitutions*. In other words, chords with this relationship are so similar to each other they may substitute for, or take the place of, one another in a harmonic progression.

The closest tritone relationship of a "dominant" 7 chord is likely to have all tones in common with the original chord with the addition of a new root, a diminished 5th away from the original root. For example, a close tritone relation of C^7 is G♭7(♭9) or G♭^{7}$\left(\begin{smallmatrix}♭9\\♭5\end{smallmatrix}\right)$.

Figure 6-42

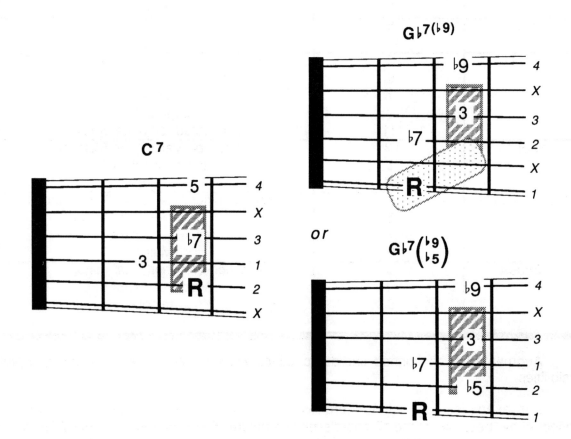

As another example, let's look at a +7($\flat$9) chord. Specifically, a close tritone relation of C+7($\flat$9) is G$\flat$9 or G$\flat$9($\sharp$11) (and vice versa).

(Note: G$\flat$9 is R 3 5 $\flat$7 9 i.e. G$\flat$ B$\flat$ D$\flat$ F$\flat$ A$\flat$ and G7($\flat$9) is R 3 5 $\flat$7 $\flat$9 i.e. G B D F A$\flat$)

Figure 6-43

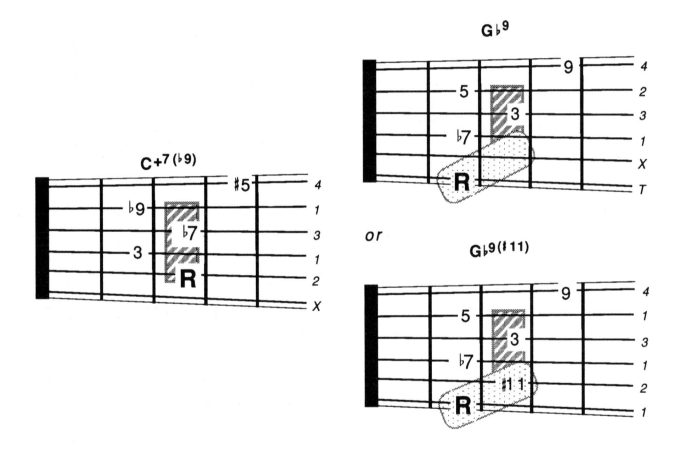

Here are some more chord forms shown with their closest tritone relative, i.e. each chord is paired with another chord having all tones in common with the original chord with the exception of a new, or different, root. Only the *implied* roots are shown in each of these chord forms, meaning, the actual roots are omitted (not played) yielding chord forms perceivable in either one of two contexts. You may find these forms, and others like them, very useful in jazz or fusion music.

Figure 6-44

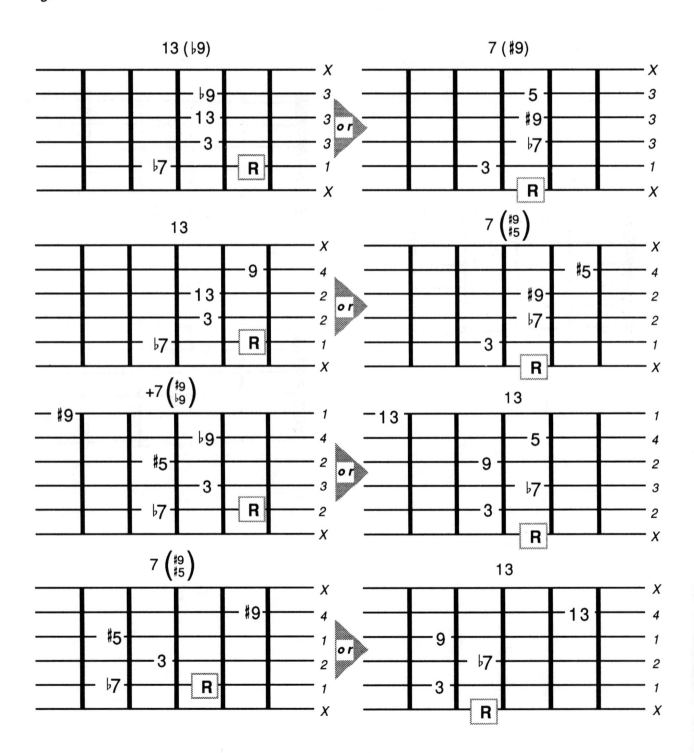

Figure 6-44 (cont'd)

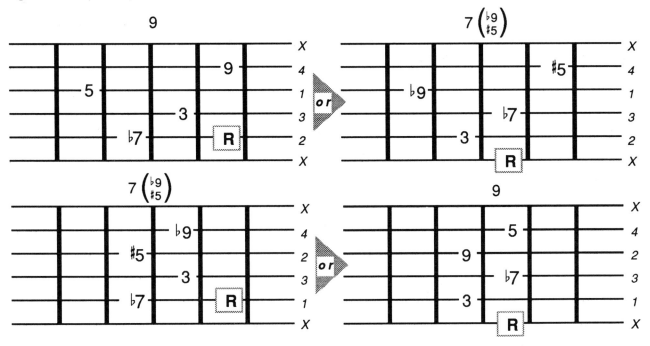

Chord Synonyms

   Chords with the same tonal content yet different perceivable roots are synonyms. Augmented chords and diminished 7 chords are two types we have mentioned already (eg. C+ = E+ = G♯+, and C∘7 = E♭∘7 = G♭∘7 = A∘7).

   "Dominant" 7 (♭5) chords (R 3 ♭5 ♭7) are in the same category as well because two 7(♭5) chords whose roots are an interval of a diminished 5th (tritone) apart share all the same chord tones. For example, A^7(♭5) (spelled A C♯ E♭ G) has the same chord tones as $E♭^7$(♭5) (spelled E♭ G B♯♯[A] D♭[C♯]).

Figure 6-45

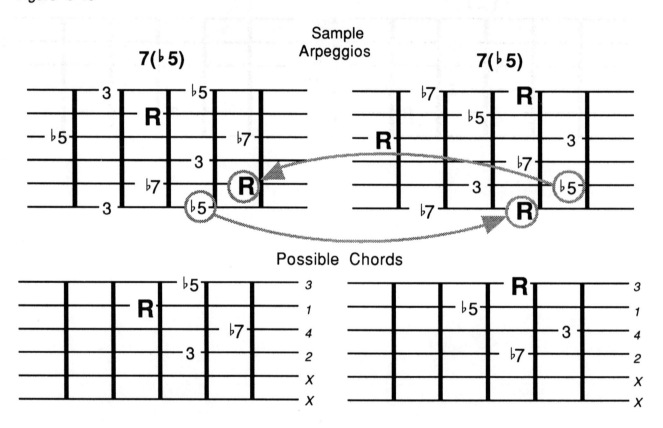

Similarly, any type of "dominant" 7 chord containing a ♭5 may be perceived as another "dominant" 7 (♭5), or ♯11, chord whose root is a diminished 5th, or tritone, away from the original root.

Figure 6-46

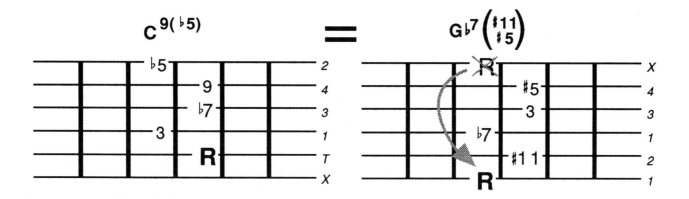

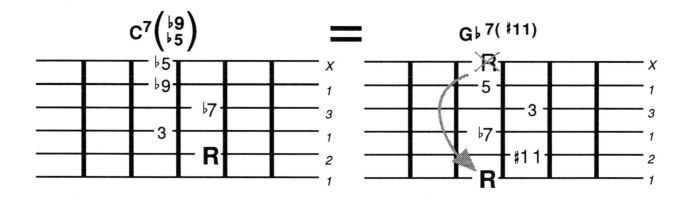

Some other chord synonyms have the same tonal content yet different root names and different suffixes as well. For example, C^6 (R 3 5 6 i.e. C E G A) has the same letter-name chord tones as A−7 (R ♭3 5 ♭7, i.e. A C E G). Observe the relationship of these two chords. The 6th of the Major 6 chord is the root of the minor 7 chord, and the ♭3rd of the minor 7 chord is the root of the Major 6 chord. From another perspective, C^6 is a 1st inversion A−7 chord (or $^{A−7}/_C$). Likewise, A−7 is a 3rd inversion C^6 chord (or $^{C6}/_A$). Knowing the relationship of synonymous chord types makes finding the synonym, or, alternate name, of a particular chord very easy.[2]

Figure 6-47

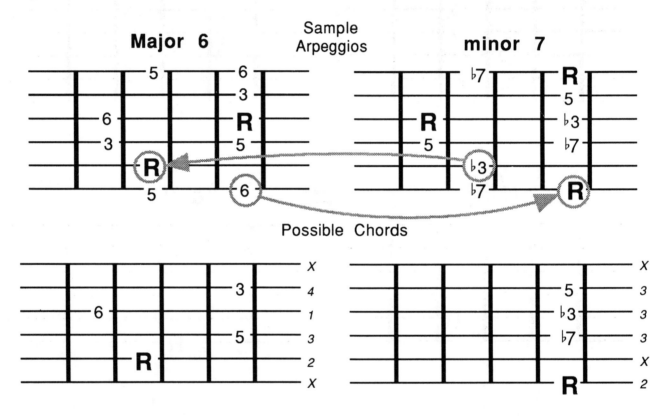

2   A chord's name is determined by its harmonic context, so you'll have to understand some theory of harmonic progression to know how to properly name a chord. (Beyond the scope of this book)

Minor 7($\flat$5) or half diminished 7 chords and minor 6 chords may also be synonymous. For example, E$\varnothing$7 (R $\flat$3 $\flat$5 $\flat$7 , that is E G B$\flat$ D) has the same tonal content as G–6 (R $\flat$3 5 6, that is, G B$\flat$ D E). The $\flat$3rd of the half diminished 7 chord is the root of the minor 6 chord, and the 6th of the minor 6 chord is the root of the half diminished 7 chord. These, and all, synonymous chords may also be perceived as different inversions of one another.

Figure 6-48

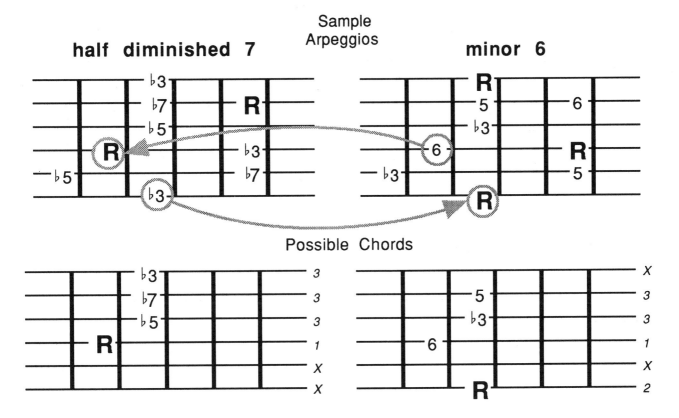

Similarly, minor 7(♯5) chords and add 9 chords may be synonymous. For example, A–7(♯5) (R ♭3 ♯5 ♭7, that is A C E♯[F] G) has the same tonal content as F^{add9} or F^2 (R 3 5 9 [or 2], that is F A C G). The ♯5 of the minor 7(♯5) chord is the root of the add 9 chord, and the 3rd of the add 9 chord is the root of the minor 7(♯5) chord.

Figure 6-49

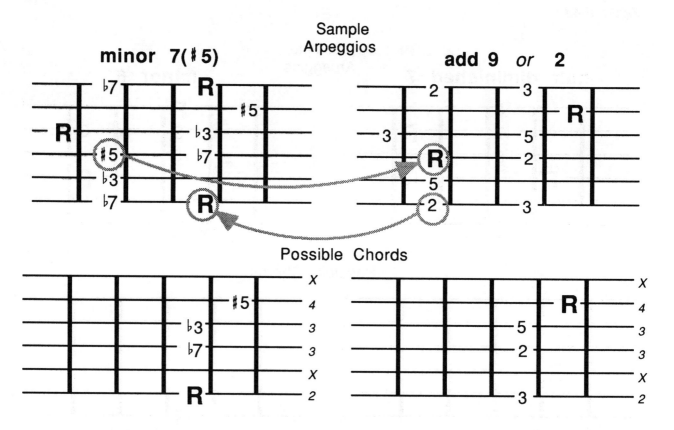

A word of caution . . . be very careful to use chords in their proper harmonic context. Even though two chords may be synonymous, having the same tonal content, one chord may be appropriate while the other is completely inappropriate. For example, F^2 (R 3 5 9 [2], that is F A C G) has the same tonal content as F/G, meaning an F major chord (F A C) with G as the lowest sounding tone. However, because the bass or lowest sounding tone in any harmonic situation most often dominates and defines the harmony, using F/G in place of, or as a substitute for, an F^2 chord can be an embarrassing error since this particular *voicing* (played in the lower register of the guitar in particular) implies a completely different harmony and confuses the harmonic intention of an F^2 chord. You'll need to study harmonic (chord) progression to better understand this.

TEST YOURSELF
CHAPTER 6

1. Show the correct horizontal transposition of the following chords making sure to account for any open strings. Indicate all fingerings.

a) Transpose this chord form a half-tone *higher*.

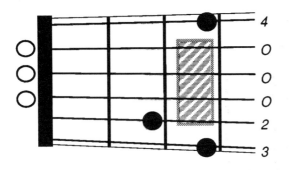 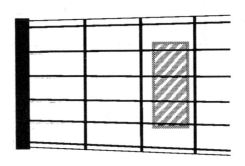

b) Transpose this chord form a half-tone *lower*:

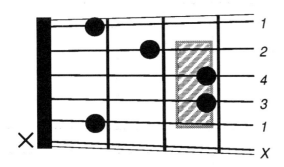 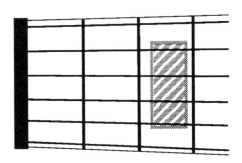

2. Transpose these chord forms vertically across the strings to create different possible chord forms with the same voicing.

a)

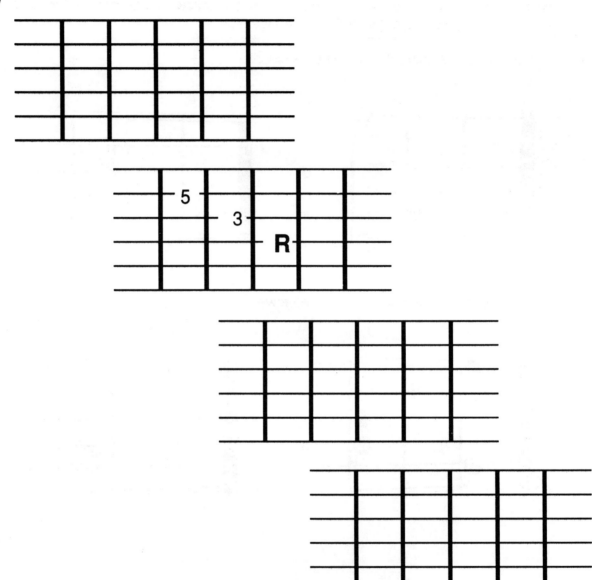

b)

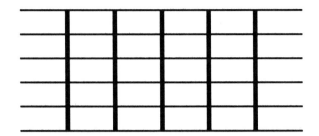

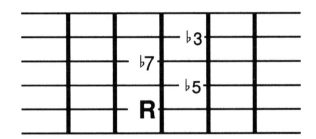

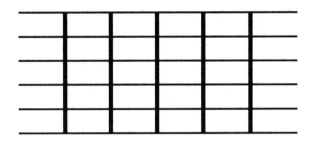

3. Find eight different voicings or forms for the "dominant" 7 chord shown below keeping within the following two octave regions:

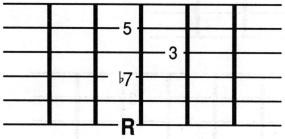

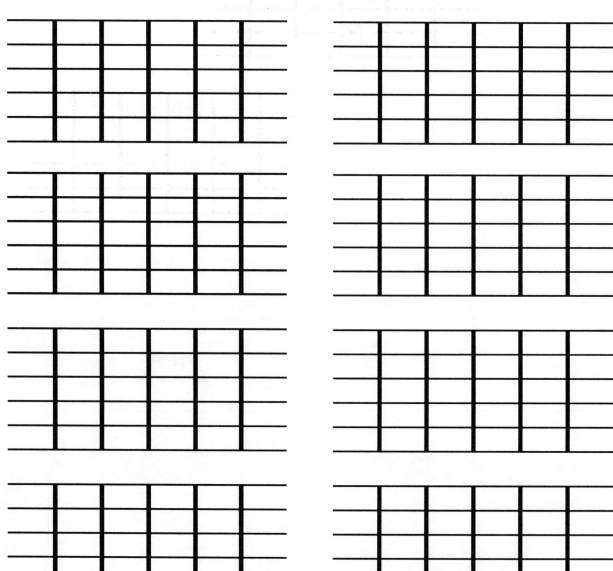

4.　Show a minor 7 chord (R ♭3 5 ♭7) in four different *second inversion* chord forms.

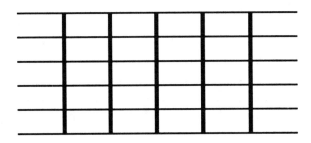

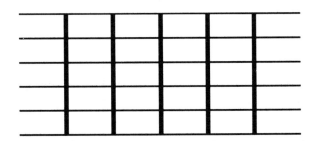

5. Make fingerboard "maps" for the following chord types in all five octave regions.

a) Major 7

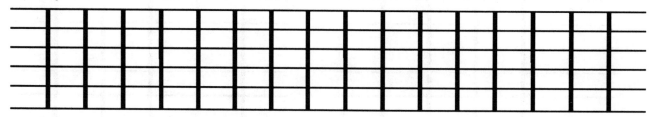

b) "Dominant" 7

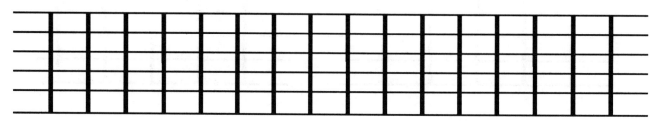

c) 13

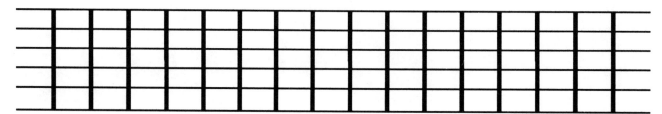

6. Make specific fingerboard "maps" for the following chords in at least five octave regions.

a) D minor 11

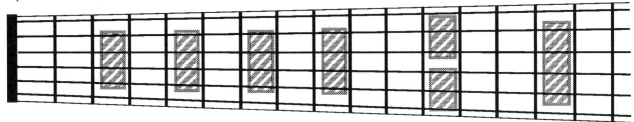

b) G♯ø7

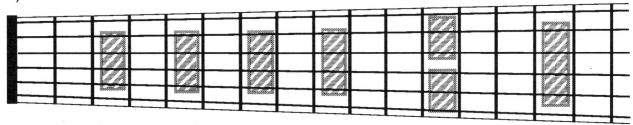

c) $C^7\left(\begin{smallmatrix}\flat 9\\\flat 5\end{smallmatrix}\right)$

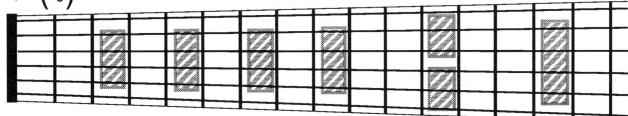

7.   Extract at least four chord forms from each of the "maps" developed in questions 6 and
      7.

a) Major 7

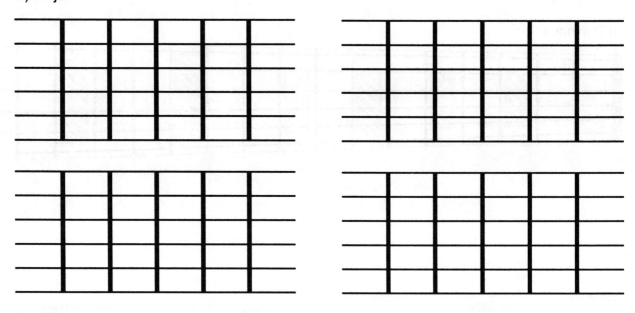

b) "Dominant" 7

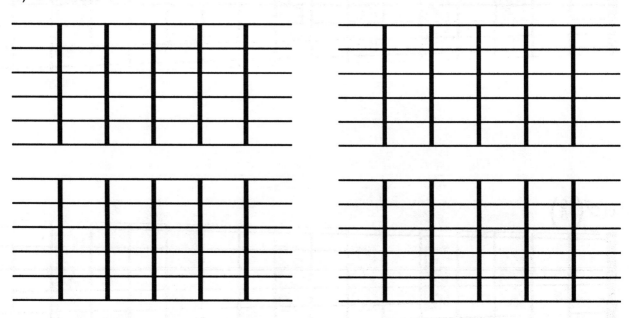

c) 13

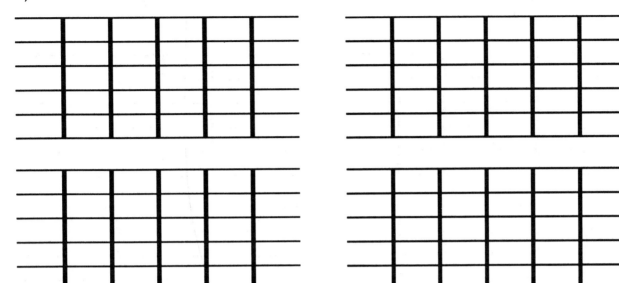

d) D minor 11

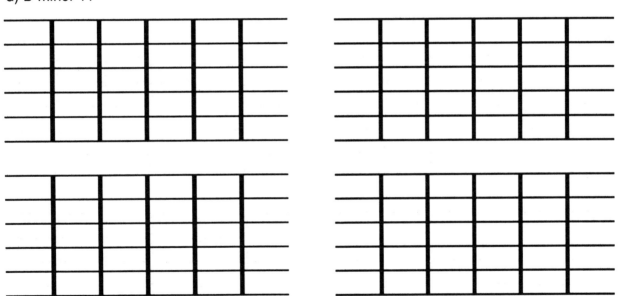

e) G#ø7

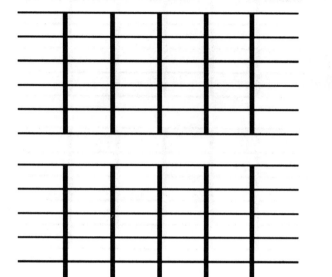
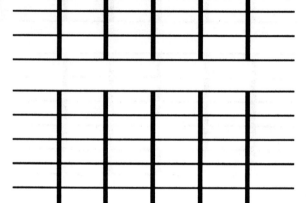

f) C$^7\left(\begin{smallmatrix}\flat 9\\ \flat 5\end{smallmatrix}\right)$

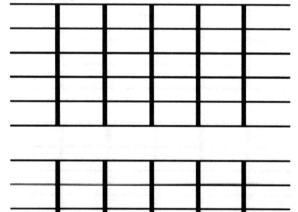
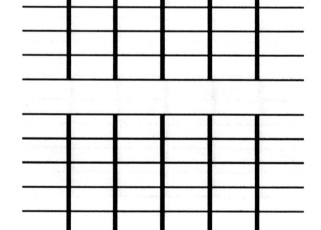

8. Arrange the following chords in:
   a) a "closed" voicing (with no interval greater than a 3rd between tones);

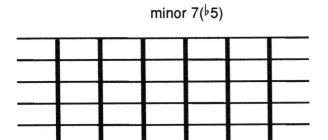

minor 7(♭5)

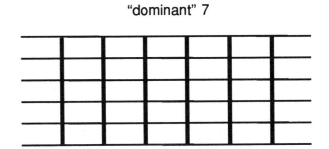

"dominant" 7

and, b) an "open" voicing.

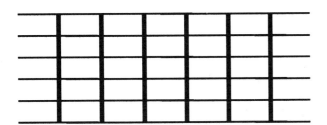

minor 7(♭5)

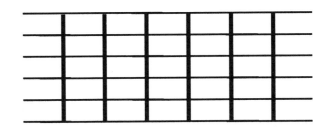

"dominant" 7

9. Give an example of a "thin" and a "thick" voicing for an "11" chord.

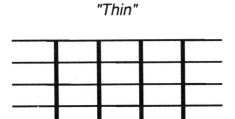

"Thin"

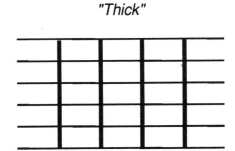

"Thick"

10. Making use of the following five string groupings, give examples of Major 7 chord forms.

'4 3 2 1'

'5 4 3 2'

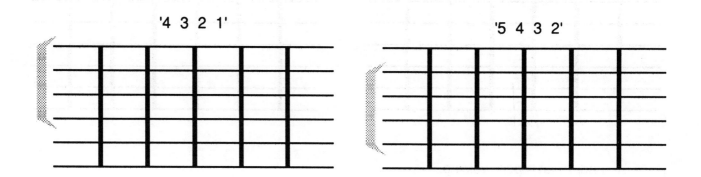

'6 5 4 3'

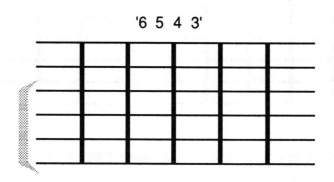

'5 3 2 1'

'6 4 3 2'

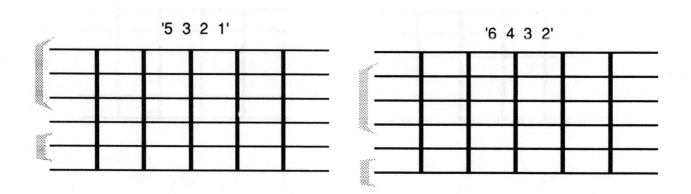

11. Beginning with the Major chord form shown below, give the most closely related chord forms for each of the following chords.

Major

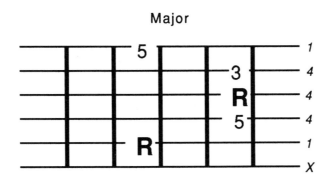

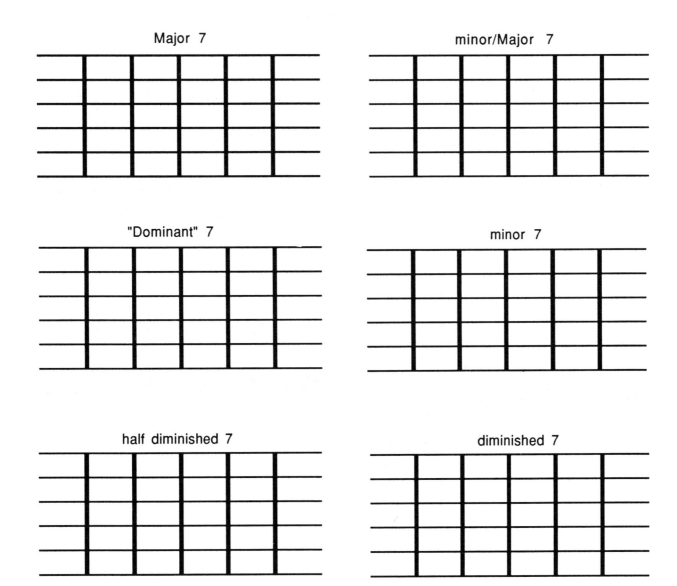

Major 7

minor/Major 7

"Dominant" 7

minor 7

half diminished 7

diminished 7

12. Give some examples of smaller chords contained within the following larger chords:

a) B♭ Major 13(♯11)

b) C minor 9

13. Give a likely tritone substitution for each of the following chords.

C⁷ (♯ 9)

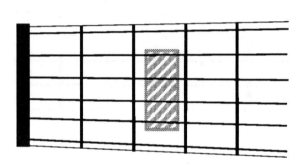

F 13

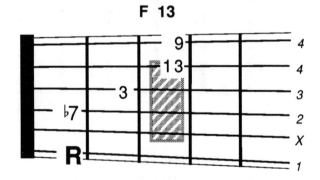

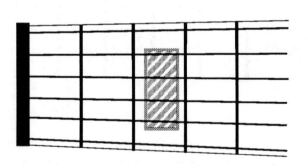

14.   a) Give four possible names for the following chord.

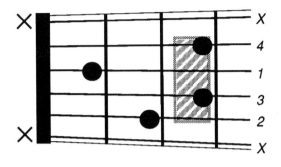

_____   _____   _____   _____

   b) Name four 7(♭9) chords implied by this one chord.

_____   _____   _____   _____

15.   a) Give three possible names for the following chord.

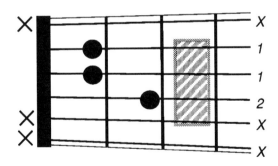

_____   _____   _____

   b) Name three minor/Major 7 chords implied by this one chord.

_____   _____   _____

16.   a) Name the chord synonymous with G♭7(♭5).

       b) Give two identical chord forms, indicating their different intervallic content, for the preceding chords.

G♭7(♭5)

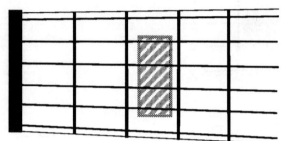

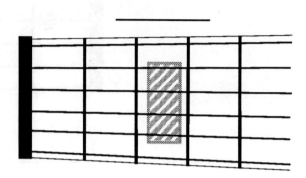

17.   Name the chords synonymous with:

       a) C♯−7

       b) G∅7

       c) A♭2

ANSWERS
TEST YOURSELF
CHAPTER 6

1.

a)

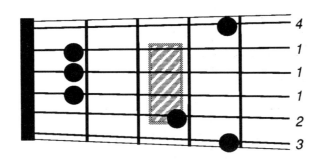

b)

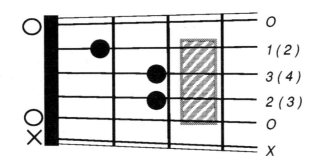

2.

a)

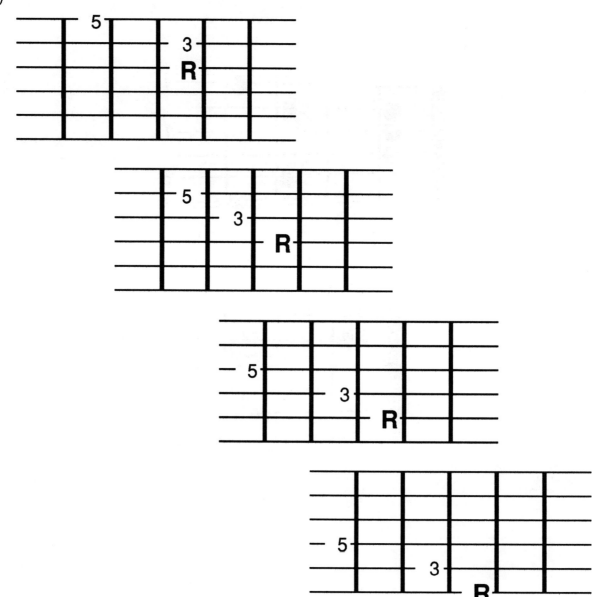

b)

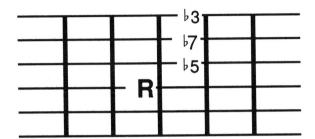

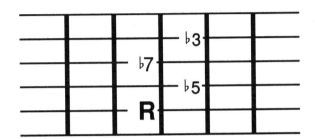

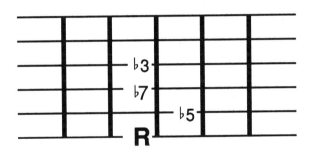

3. (There are more than eight correct answers.)

4. (There are more than four correct answers.)

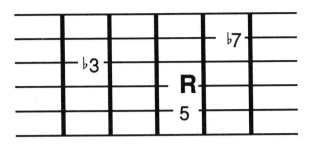 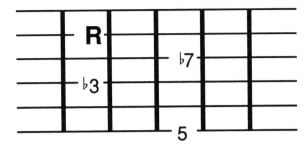

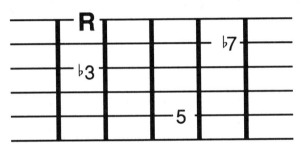 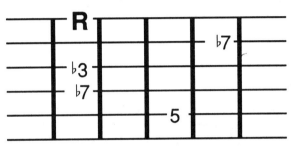

5. a)

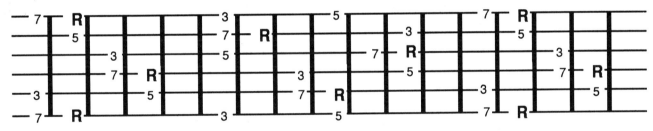

b)

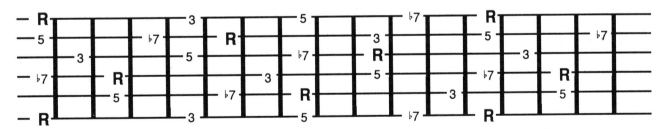

c)

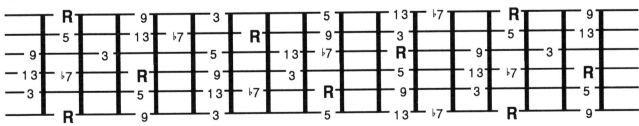

6.

a)

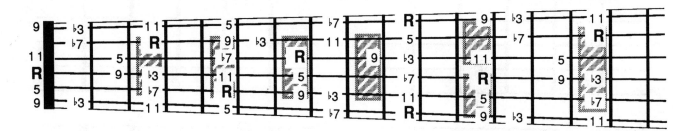

b)

c)

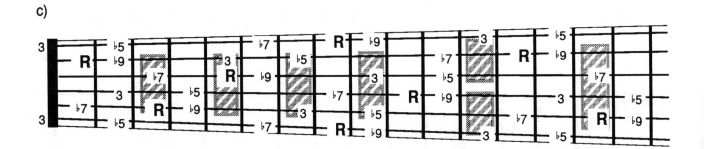

7. (There are more than four correct answers for each chord.)

a) Major 7

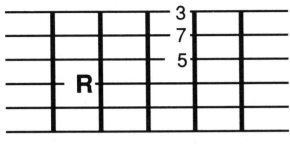 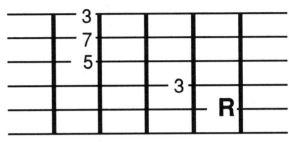

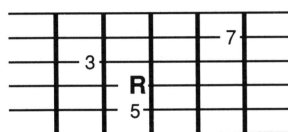 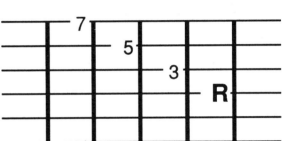

b) "Dominant" 7

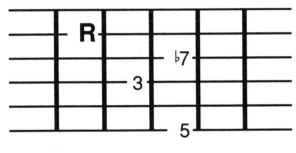

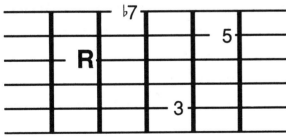 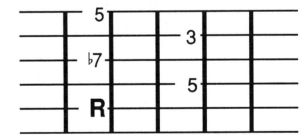

c) 13

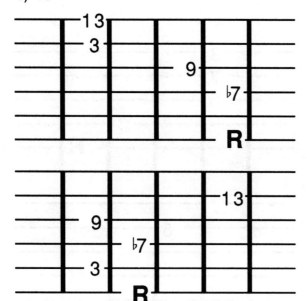

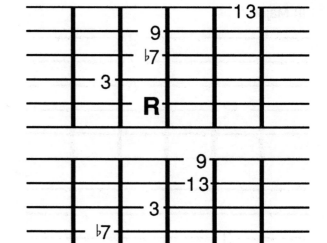

d) D minor 11

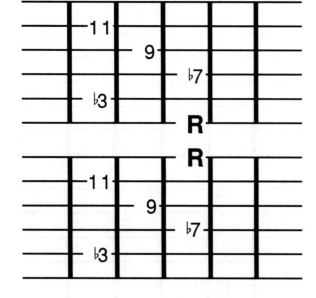

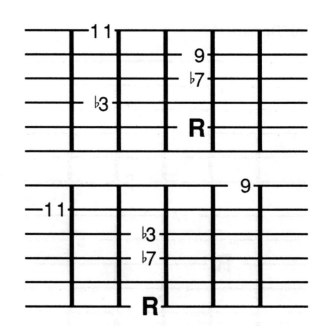

e) G#⌀7

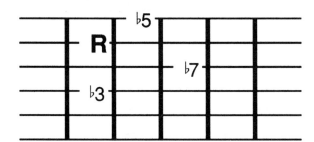

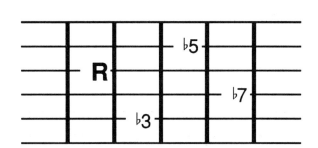

f) C⁷(♭9 ♭5)

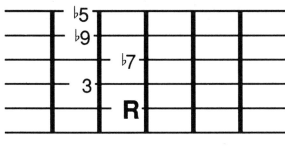

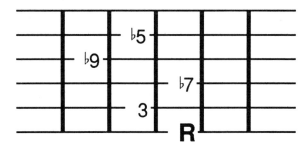

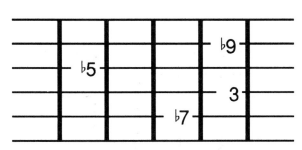

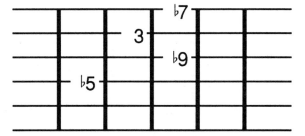

8. (There is more than one correct answer for each chord.)

a)

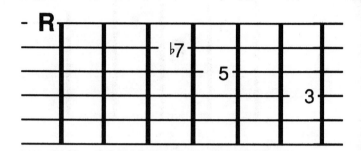

b)

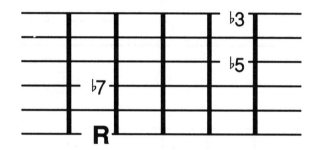
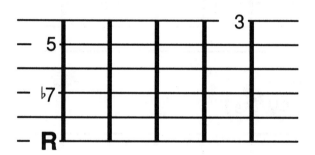

9. (There is more than one correct answer.)

"Thin"

"Thick"

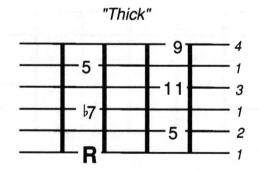

10.   (There is more than one correct answer for each group of strings.)

'4 3 2 1'

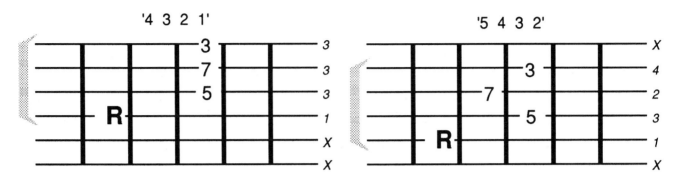

'5 4 3 2'

'6 5 4 3'

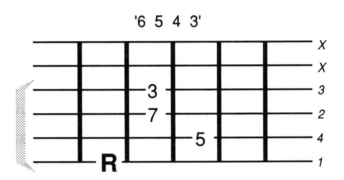

'5 3 2 1'

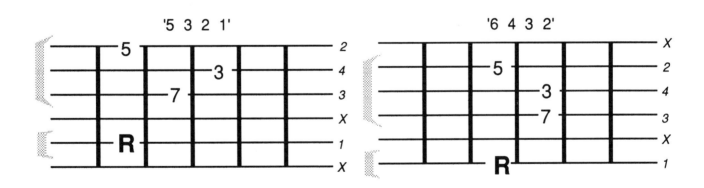

'6 4 3 2'

11.

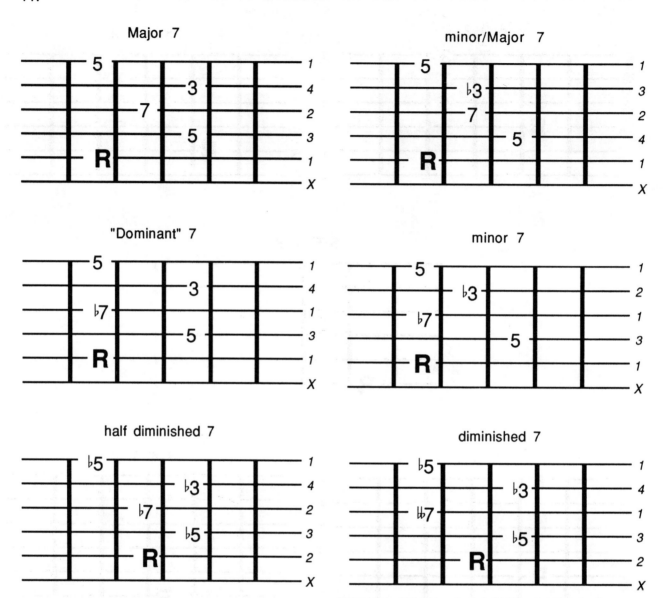

Major 7

minor/Major 7

"Dominant" 7

minor 7

half diminished 7

diminished 7

12.

a) D minor, D minor 7, D minor 9, D minor 11, F Major, F Major 7, F Major 9, A minor, A minor 7, C Major.

b) E♭ Major, E♭ Major 7, G minor.

13.

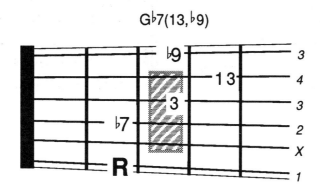

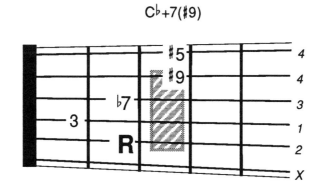

14. a) B○7, D○7, F○7, A♭○7

b) B♭7(♭9), E7(♭9), D♭7(♭9), G7(♭9)

15. a) E+, G♯+, C+

b) F m/M7, A m/M7, C♯ m/M7

16. a) C7($\flat$5)

    b)

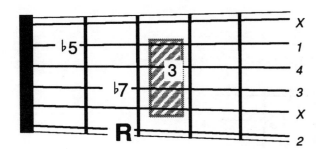

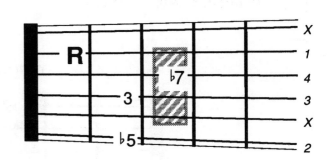

17. a) E^6

    b) B$\flat$m^6

    c) Cm^7($\sharp$5)

CHAPTER 7
Advanced Chord Construction Concepts

Poly-chords

   A poly-chord consists of any two or more distinct chordal units (most often triads, or possibly four tone chords or larger) sounding simultaneously; or, in other words, any two or more distinct chords played as one chord. Therefore, the identifiable sound of a poly-chord is produced by both the separateness and distinctness of more than one resonant chord structure, and the sonority of these multiple structures sounding as one.

   From a tertian perspective however, the concept of poly-chords may be understood within the realm of chord plurality and chord synonymy since the term poly-chord describes both a smaller chord "contained" within a larger chord, and a chord with a particular tonal content yet with another possible name or description. Consequently, an understanding of poly-chords provides a different way of perceiving, and different means of constructing, chords.

   While tertian chords have acquired a host of, sometimes differing, slang names and shorthand suffixes from musicians because of their wide use in popular music, poly-chords and other varieties of chords to be discussed in the remainder of this chapter are neither necessarily *conceived* in, nor *intended* for, the tertian realm and have no such slang names or suffixes in common use. Consequently, a venture to define poly-chords or other varieties of chords conceived outside the realm of tertian harmony in tertian terms, with slang names and suffixes, is an erroneous endeavor. Since, however, "main-stream" and popular music uses tertian harmony almost exclusively, an attempt is made to show how poly-chords or other varieties of chords might be understood from a tertian perspective; nevertheless this attempt has its practical limits for the aforementioned reason.

   In purest form, a poly-chord consists of two distinct, separate triads. For example, this $G7\left(\begin{smallmatrix}\sharp11\\ \flat9\end{smallmatrix}\right)$ chord (R 3 5 ♭7 ♭9 ♯11, i.e. G B D F A♭ C♯) may be seen as two triads, G major (G B D) and D♭ major (D♭ F A♭), in combination. The shorthand used by musicians to convey a poly-chord is to place one chord directly on top of the other separated by a horizontal line; thus the above mentioned chord is written: $\frac{D♭}{G}$.

Figure 7-1

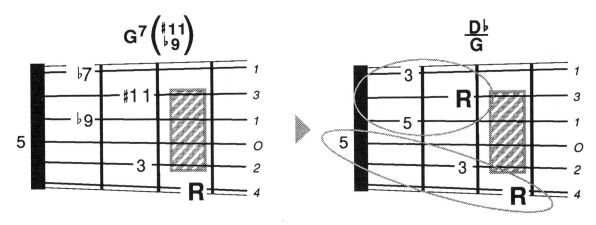

Likewise, G Maj 7$\left(\begin{smallmatrix}\sharp 11\\ \sharp 9\end{smallmatrix}\right)$ may be seen as two triads: G Major and F♯ (or G♭) Major.

Figure 7-2

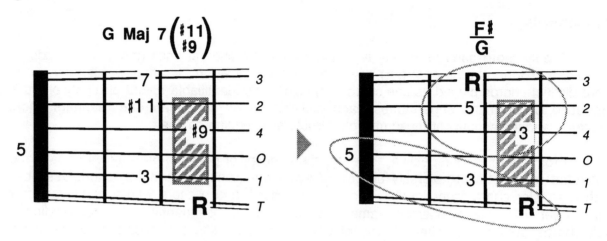

Sometimes, however, both triads of the poly-chord have one tone in common. In such cases, guitarists usually omit the common tone from the bottom triad for a more economical fingering since that same tone is duplicated in the top triad.[1] Observe the next two examples.

Figure 7-3

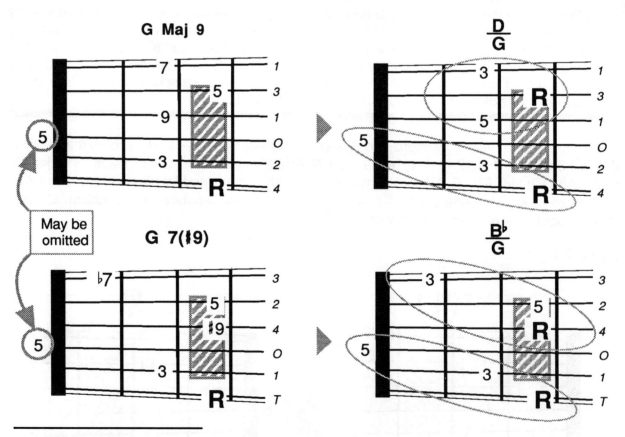

---

[1] Constructing a poly-chord with more than one tone in common among both triads lessens the poly-chord's aural effect. Consequently, such chords are better perceived in a purely tertian context and written in ordinary form.

The next most common practice is to use a triad with an added 7th degree as the bottom chord (Major 7, minor 7, and most often the "dominant" 7). The 5th is often omitted from the bottom chord. For example,

Figure 7-4

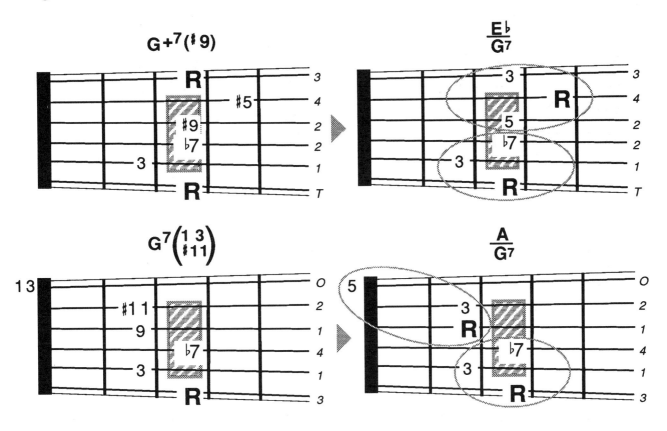

The term poly-chord becomes strained when applied to chords with an omitted 3rd in the bottom chord. The 9sus4 chord is an example of this, shown in Figure 7-5 as "poly-chord-like" as possible. Consequently, chords of this type are not well named as poly-chords.

Figure 7-5

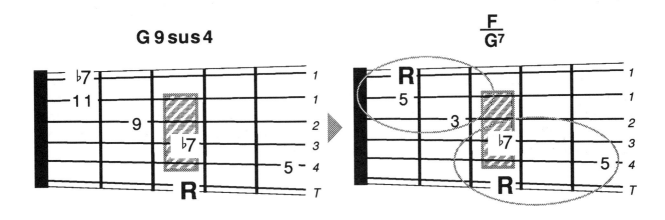

Chords like $^{Dm}/_C$ or $^A/_G$ are *not* poly-chords, but rather 3rd inversions of D−7 and A⁷ chords, respectively.

Figure 7-6

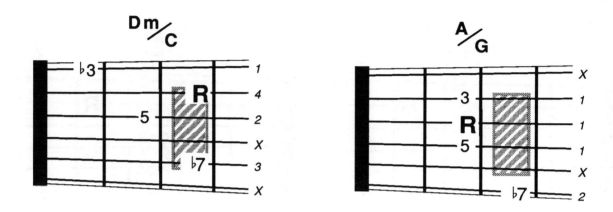

Chords like $^{Dm}/_B$ and $^{B\flat}/_G$ are also *not* poly-chords, but rather an alternate way of writing Bø7 and G−7.

Figure 7-7

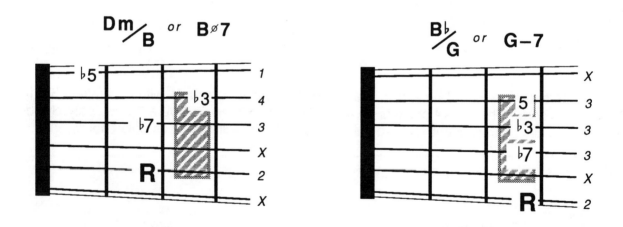

Many chords with five tones or more may be understood as poly-chords. Carefully observing a chord's tones may reveal its plurality, while experimenting with different combinations of a chord's tones may possibly unveil a poly-chord structure. From another perspective, systematically superimposing any series of chords upon another stationary chord may generate an array of useful poly-chords to choose from for a given situation.

Quartal Chords

Up to this point we have dealt with chords built on intervals of a 3rd from one tone to the next, called tertian, or triadic, harmony. Quartal harmony describes chords built on intervals of a 4th from one tone to the next. Chords built on 4ths may be understood and applied within the realm of tertian harmony; or stated another way, chords built on 3rds may be manipulated in such a way as to create quartal harmony. The result is a unique identifiable sound used frequently in jazz and fusion music.

Let's begin by building a 4-tone quartal chord with C as the root. Each chord tone will be a perfect 4th ($2\frac{1}{2}$ steps) apart. Observe the pattern of these tones on the fingerboard.

Figure 7-8

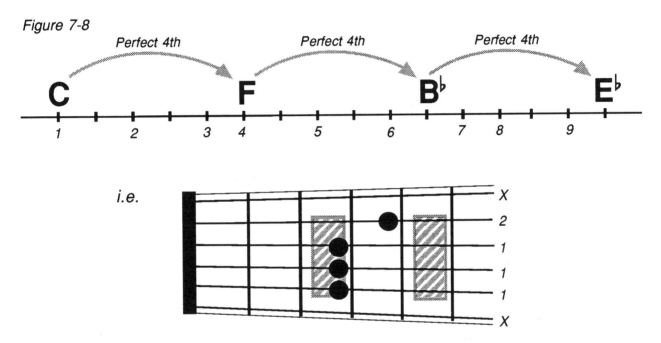

Similar to the augmented and diminished 7 chords with tones equidistant from one to the other resulting in the possibility of any chord tone being perceived as the root, quartal chords may likewise be perceived from several different tertian perspectives:

1) C−7 (add 11);

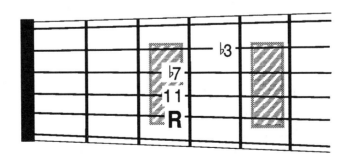

2) F^{sus 4} (second inversion);

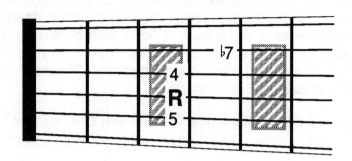

3) B♭^{sus} 4/2 (first inversion);

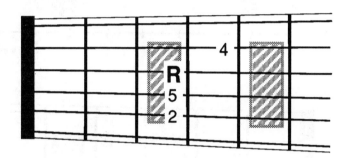

4) E♭6/9 (no 3rd);

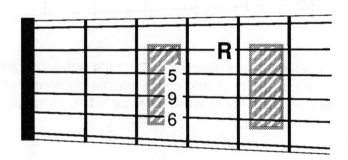

or, 5) A♭6/9 (no root).

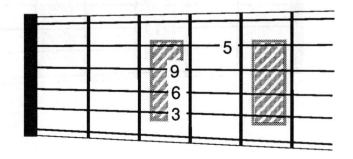

Smaller, three tone, quartal chords are also possible, and very useful, with even greater tertian potential. Extracted from the above quartal structure, Figure 7-9 , for example, illustrates a possible quartal chord implying all the preceding tertian chords with the addition of C^{7}sus4 (no 5th), or perhaps G^{7}sus4($\sharp$9)(no root).

Figure 7-9

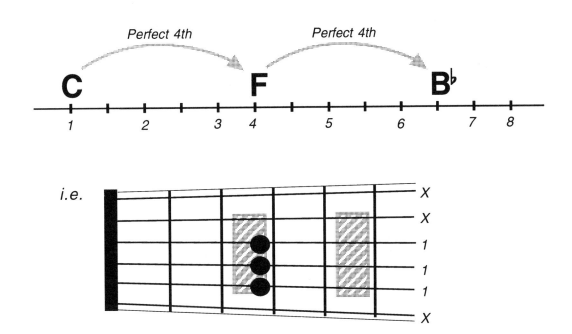

Quartal chords in general are most characteristic and resonant structured as a series of perfect 4th intervals. Inverting these chords in such a way as to incur intervals other than 4ths, will, in most cases, lessen the quartal effect, even though the chord's tonal content has not changed. On the contrary, inverting quartal chords to produce larger, more resonant, intervals of 5ths (sometimes called *quintal* chords, i.e. chords built by intervals of 5ths) produces a more broad, open effect desirous in some situations. Larger quartal chords with five or more tones are possible, as well as quartal chords containing augmented 4th intervals, yielding increasingly dissonant effects with more complex tertian implications.

Secundal Chords

Thus far we have discussed chords built within two categories: 3rds and 4ths. The other remaining category is chords built by 2nds, or secundal chords. These, however, are more rare, and even more difficult to execute on the guitar. [2]

Unless a guitarist has abnormally long, or elastic, fingers, the largest root position secundal chord playable on the guitar contains no more than three tones, assuming the standard tuning is used (or four tones if an open string is incorporated).

Contrary to quartal chords, secundal chords are more dissonant by nature. Consequently, major and minor 2nds or their inversions (7ths) are all readily acceptable, though the secundal chords containing more major intervals are more consonant, while those containing more minor intervals are more dissonant.

Similar to quartal chords, secundal chords may be understood and applied within the realm of tertian harmony. Here are some examples:

Figure 7-10

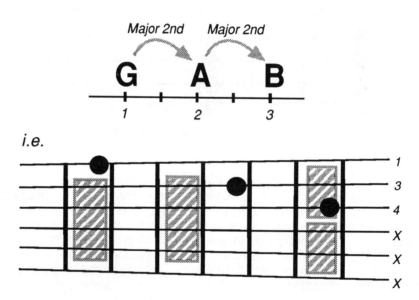

This chord may be perceived as:

1) G^2;

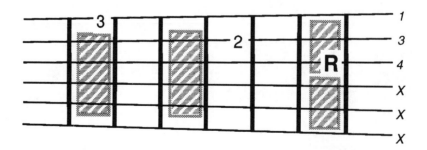

---

[2]   Chords built by 5ths, 6ths and 7ths are commonly thought of as intervallic inversions of 4ths, 3rds and 2nds, respectively. Consequently, they do not constitute another category and are not discussed.

2) Em add 4;

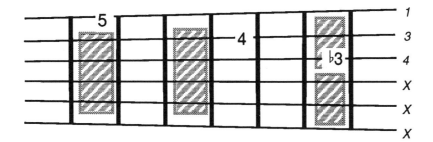

or 3) A^9 . (...just to name a few)

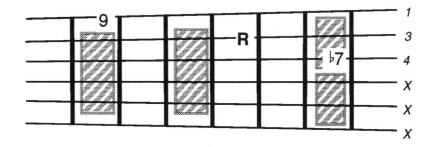

Here's an extreme dissonant example of a secundal chord:

Figure 7-11

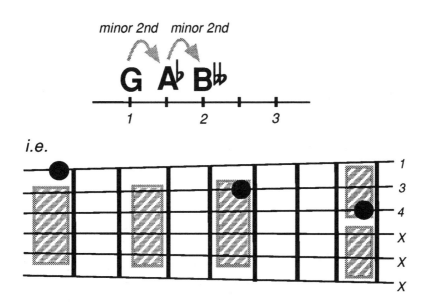

You'll really have to stretch the boundaries of tertian harmony to find an implied (tertian) relation for the above secundal chord. Consequently, the most useful secundal chords for use in tertian contexts have at least one major 2nd interval.

Pandiatonicism

The Major scale is an example of a *diatonic* scale, meaning it has a "gravitational center" or place of rest called the tonic, whose other scale members have varying degrees of relaxation and tension as they progress toward or away from this place of rest. By contrast, any scale (most characteristically, a diatonic scale) may be treated *pandiatonically*; that is, each scale member's function regarding its degree of relaxation or tension may be removed, treating each scale tone with "functional *equality*", void of any true tonic or gravitation toward any scale tone.

In a harmonic context, any scale, or collection of tones, may be used as a foundation for harmony, i.e. the construction of chords (and chord progressions), the same way the major scale is used. Within pandiatonicism however, since scale tones have functional equality beyond the tendencies for tension and relaxation and are without any gravitation toward a tonic, there is *no harmonic progression* (i.e. no changing from one chord to another). In essence, the entire scale is treated as a chord in itself; any combination of tones selected from the scale are available for any conceivable rhythmic or melodic use; yet there is no harmonic progression. The result is varied rhythmic and melodic motion within motionless, or stationary, harmony.

In jazz/fusion music, as one example of how pandiatonicism is applied, a chord substitution may be taken to such an extreme as to utilize any quantity or combination of tones from an entire scale for creating "new chords" (or "chord substitutions") within an otherwise stationary chord of any type. Suppose within a particular harmonic situation, e.g. the "key" of C Major (i.e. the portion of music whose melodic and harmonic foundation is the C Major scale) there arises a C Major 7 chord. If this harmonic situation is handled pandiatonically, the entire C Major scale may be treated as the chord at hand, while "C Major 7" may be considered one of many possible pandiatonic combinations of tones derived from that scale.

Though the above musical scenario describes a pandiatonic approach to chord construction, the actual application of resulting chords tends to gravitate toward a tonal center if applied in a tonal melodic environment; the ultimate effect, whether purely pandiatonic or otherwise, is determined by the composer's (guitarist's) choice of chordal structures and harmonic/melodic direction.

Figure 7-12 shows the tones of the C Major scale across three octave regions on the fingerboard.

Figure 7-12

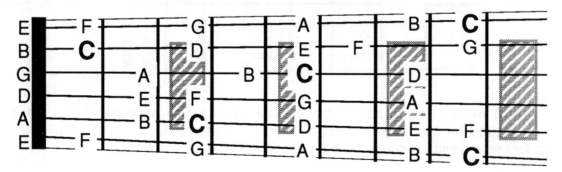

In addition, specific harmonic motifs may be chosen within a pandiatonic setting; that is, tones may be assembled into tertian, quartal, secundal or other intervallic structures for an added textural dimension, though larger chord structures without any root feel are most characteristic. In the harmonic situation described above, quartal structures, or mostly quartal structures with an occasional 3rd, are used as a harmonic motif since they are idiomatic to jazz and fusion music as displayed in Figure 7-13, though any conceivable combination of tones or structure is feasible.

Figure 7-13

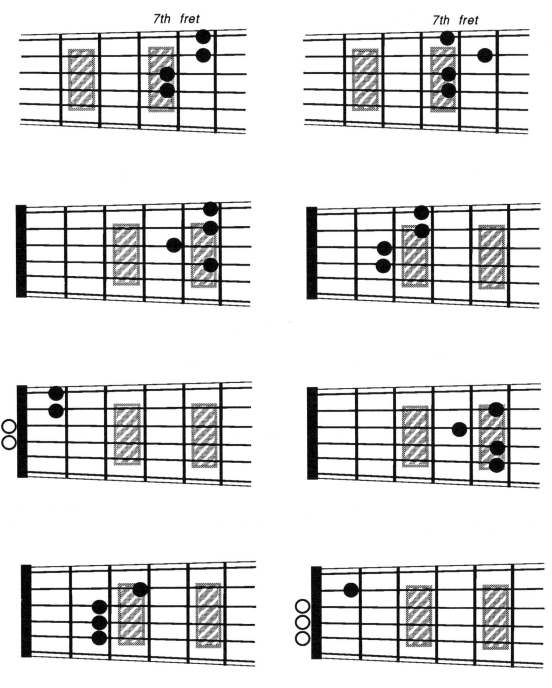

Compound Chords

Taking the idea of intervallic couplings a step further, *compound* chords are formed by the select combination of three or more various intervals. On the contrary, tertian, quartal and secundal chords are founded upon a particular intervallic distance (i.e. 2nds, 3rds or 4ths and their respective inversions); the mixed intervals arising from the inversion of these chords do not constitute compound chords. Compound chords, are constructed one select interval of any variety upon another, without any root foundation or adherence to any of the former intervallic schemes (i.e. intervals of 2nds, 3rds or 4ths etc...). Once again, tension and relaxation are achieved by composing intervals with varying degrees of dissonance and consonance.

Figure 7-15 gives an example of a compound chord.

Figure 7-15

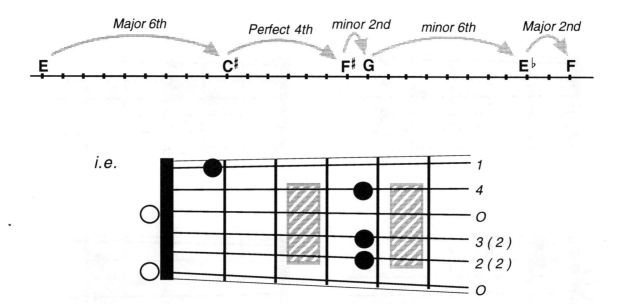

In this example, a series of intervals are selected with varying degrees of consonance and dissonance. There is no root, nor is there any practical reason to explain this chord as tertian or anything other than compound.

Chords Derived From Scales

When studying harmonic progressions in tonal music, the vast majority of chords are truly understood as scale derived. That is, in the tertian chords explained in Chapter 3 for example, there is no haphazard assemblage of 3rds, rather, the basic foundational triads and chords that follow evolve from a systematic construction from some type of diatonic scale and alterations therefrom. Specifically, in order to construct a series of chords from a scale, upon each scale tone is superimposed two or more adjacent scale tones set apart by a distance based upon a particular scheme of 2nds, 3rds, 4ths or otherwise. Each resulting chord has a varying degree of relaxation and tension gravitating toward the tonic chord. Consequently, the relationships among chords in this type of scale-derived chord "family" form the basis of harmonic progression.

For example, Figure 7-17 illustrates the creation of a family of three-tone chords derived from a C major scale with a tertian approach.

Figure 7-17

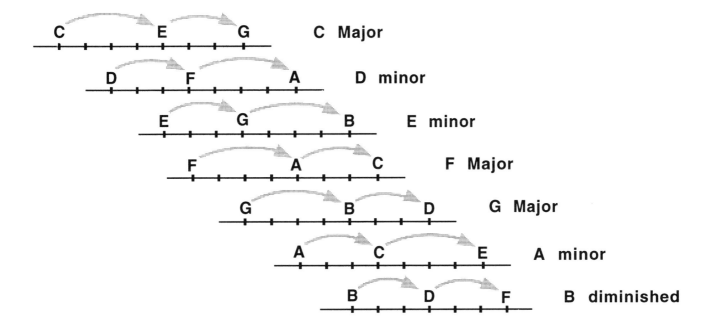

For variety, the superimposition of scale tones using a particular intervallic scheme (of 2nds, 3rds, or 4ths...) may continue beyond the foundational triad producing chords with four or more tones; or, other scale tones may be added, omitted, altered or suspended as displayed in Chapter 3.

For a complete understanding of chords the student is encouraged to study music theory and harmonic progression in its entirety. In essence, there are many types of scales: diatonic, nondiatonic (without a tonal center), synthetic, and more; once one understands the principles governing chord construction from basic diatonic scales, the same principles may be applied to other scales, or collections of tones, (and every modal scale form) to build a variety of chords in an assortment of harmonic contexts.

TEST YOURSELF
CHAPTER 7

1.   a) Voice the following chords as polychords and name them as such.

$G^7 \begin{bmatrix} 13 \\ 11 \\ \flat 9 \end{bmatrix}$ _____

F#–11   _____

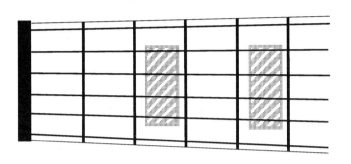

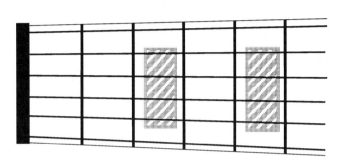

    b) Name the following chords:

_____

_____

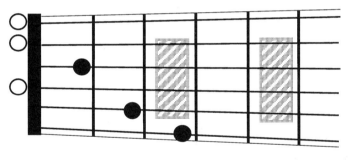

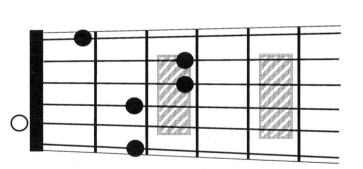

_____

_____

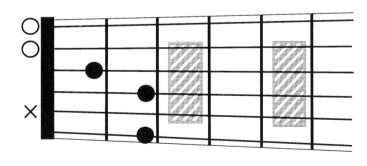

2.   Voice the following chords as quartal structures:

A♭7sus4

G–11

B♭Maj.13(♯11)

D♭–11

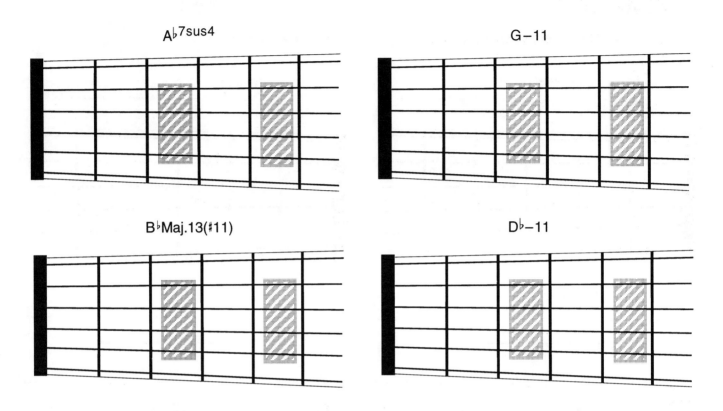

3.   a) Harmonize the tone in the following diagram as a four tone secundal chord.

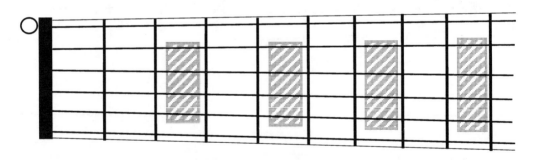

b) Harmonize the tone in the following diagram as a three tone secundal chord with at least one Major 2nd.

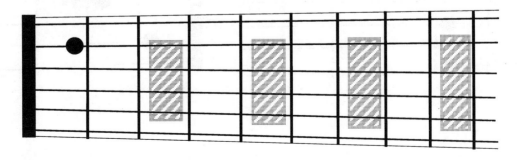

4.   Observe the F13 chord below. Treating this chord's harmonic environment in a pandiatonic manner, give some four tone chordal structures making use of the top four tones of the F13 chord as a structural motif. (Hint: The appropriate tones are found in the B♭ Major scale.)

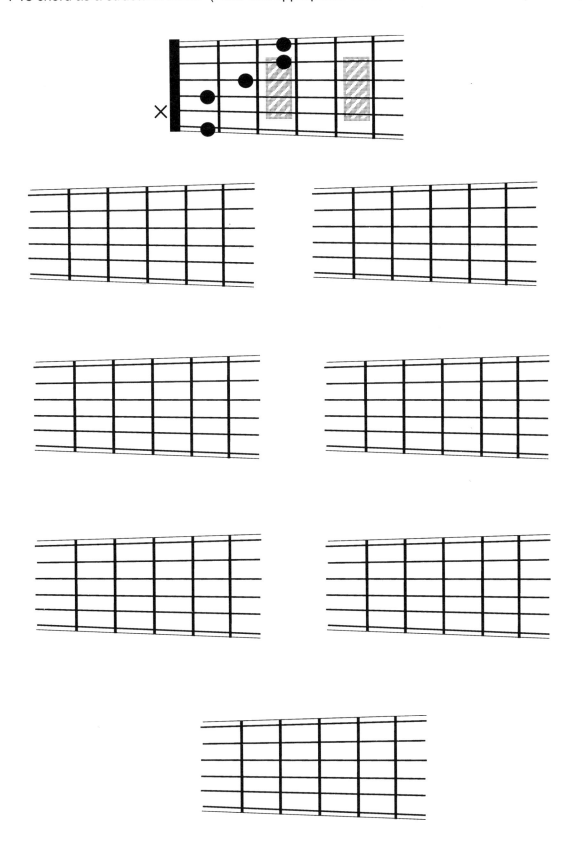

5. Create the entire family of chords for the following major scales adhering to the given parameters:

a) B♭ :   four-tone tertian chord structures;

b) G :   five-tone tertian chord structures;

c) D♭ :   four-tone quartal chord structures. (Do not attempt to give implied tertian chord suffixes.)

ANSWERS
TEST YOURSELF
CHAPTER 7

1.   a)

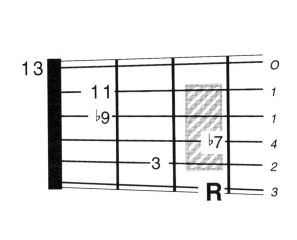

$\dfrac{A^{\flat+}}{G^7}$

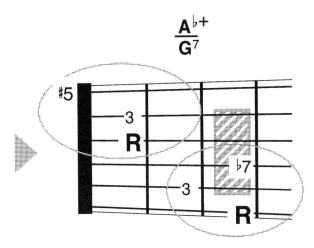

$\dfrac{F}{G^{-7}}$

b)

$\dfrac{E}{G}$

$\dfrac{B^\flat}{F{-}7}$

F#11

B♭Major7

2.

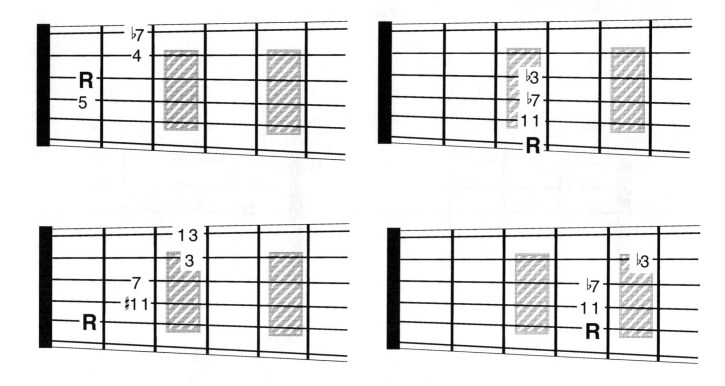

3.   a) (There is more than one correct answer.)

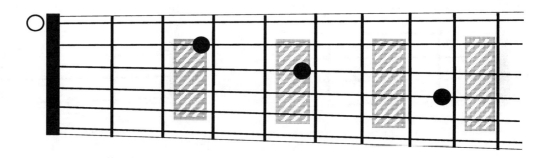

b) (There is more than one correct answer.)

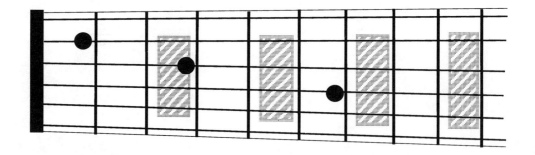

4.

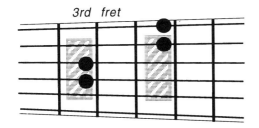

3rd fret

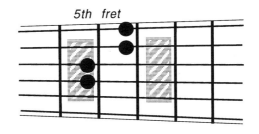

5th fret

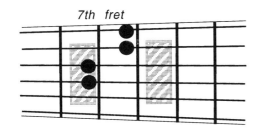

7th fret

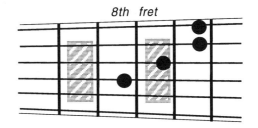

8th fret

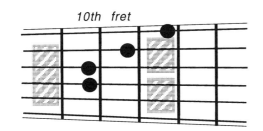

10th fret

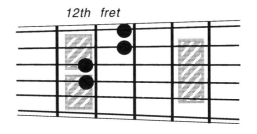

12th fret

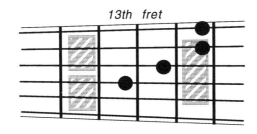

13th fret

5.

a)

Bb	D	F	A	:	Bb Major 7
C	Eb	G	Bb	:	C minor 7
D	F	A	C	:	D minor 7
Eb	G	Bb	D	:	Eb Major 7
F	A	C	Eb	:	F "Dominant" 7
G	Bb	D	F	:	G minor 7
A	C	Eb	G	:	A half diminished 7

b)

G	B	D	F#	A	:	G Major 9
A	C	E	G	B	:	A minor 9
B	D	F#	A	C	:	B minor 9
C	E	G	B	D	:	C Major 9
D	F#	A	C	E	:	D 9
E	G	B	D	F#	:	E minor 9
F#	A	C	E	G	:	F# minor 9 (b5)

c)

Db	Gb	C	F
Eb	Ab	Db	Gb
F	Bb	Eb	Ab
Gb	C	F	Bb
Ab	Db	Gb	C
Bb	Eb	Ab	Db
C	F	Bb	Eb

Appendixes

1.   Left hand finger symbols

Finger	Symbol
Thumb	T
Index	1
Middle	2
Ring (Annular)	3
Pinky	4

2.   Fingerboard Diagrams

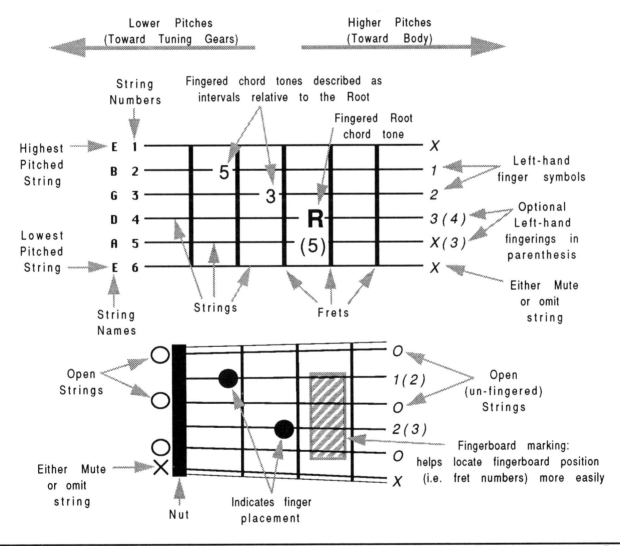

Note: Fingerboard chord tones are shown *behind* the fret where they are actually played. To produce a pure sounding tone on the guitar, a string must be depressed slightly behind the fret (toward the tuning gears), not directly on top of the fret.
    Fingerboard location in the top diagram is changeable (i.e. the letter-name of the Root determines the letter-name of the chord, scale or arpeggio allowing the illustrated finger placements to move to any fret) though relative finger placement (one finger's relative location to another) is as shown; the bottom diagram is intended as an exact graphic representation of fingerboard location and finger placement.

3. Scale and Arpeggio Fingerboard Diagrams

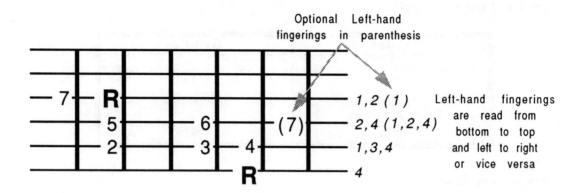

4. Abbreviations and Symbols

Abbreviation	Meaning
M *or* Ma *or* Maj	Major
m *or* mi *or* min	Minor
A *or* au *or* aug	Augmented
d *or* dim	Diminished
P	Perfect

Symbols	Meaning
Δ	Major 7 chord
7	"dominant" 7 chord
–	minor
+	augmented
o	diminished
ø	half-diminished
Chord number with slash drawn through it: e.g. 7 *or* 13	Chord contains a *Major 7th* scale degree

APPENDIX 2: *A Method for Tuning the Guitar*

1. To tune the guitar to standard pitch, tune the 6th string (E) to another instrument or device that generates or measures standard pitch;

    e.g. either a)   a *TUNED* piano;

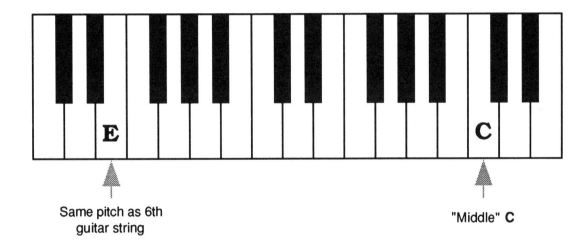

    Same pitch as 6th   "Middle" C
    guitar string

    b)   a *tuning fork* tuned to E (the "E" generated by most tuning forks is two octaves higher than the 6th guitar string) or a *pitch pipe* (pitch pipes for the guitar give the pitch of all six guitar strings, yet are not the most accurate means of tuning the instrument though they suffice for beginners); or,

    c)   an electronic tuner (these may be used to tune the entire instrument).

    NOTE: *If you are unable to use one of these means to obtain standard pitch, you may proceed with steps 2 through 6 anyway; just realize that each guitar string will be tuned relative one another, yet the instrument as a whole will (most likely) not be tuned to standard pitch.*

2. Make the 5th string (A) sound identical in pitch to the tone at the 5th fret of the 6th string (E).

3. Make the 4th string (D) sound identical in pitch to the tone at the 5th fret of the 5th string (A).

4. Make the 3rd string (G) sound identical in pitch to the tone at the 5th fret of the 4th string (D).

5. Make the 2nd string (B) sound identical in pitch to the tone at the *4th* fret of the 3rd string (G).

6. Make the 1st string (E) sound identical in pitch to the tone at the 5th fret of the 2nd string (B).

APPENDIX 3: *Major Scale Patterns*

Five Octave Regions

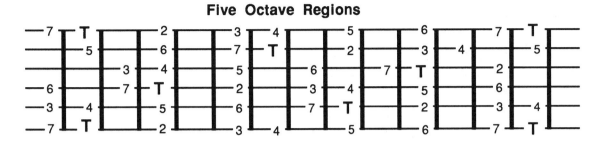

Series of Five Major Scale Patterns

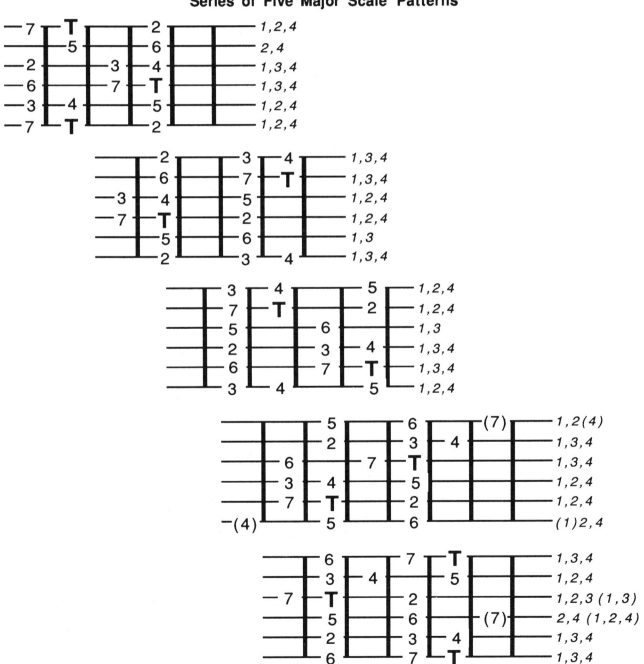

Series of Seven Major Scale Patterns

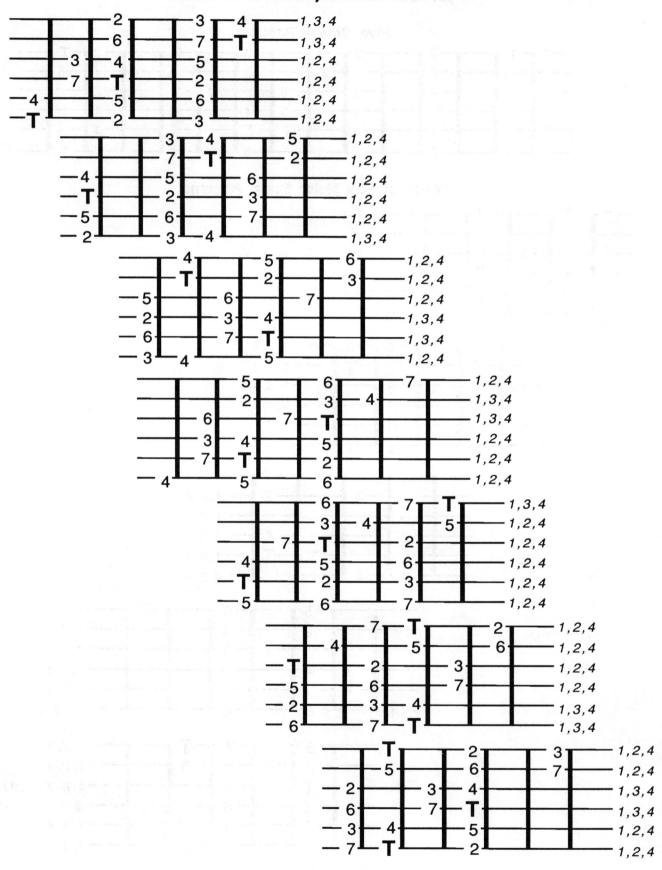

APPENDIX 4: *Some Basic Arpeggio Patterns*

Major 7 Arpeggios   **"Dominant" 7 Arpeggios**

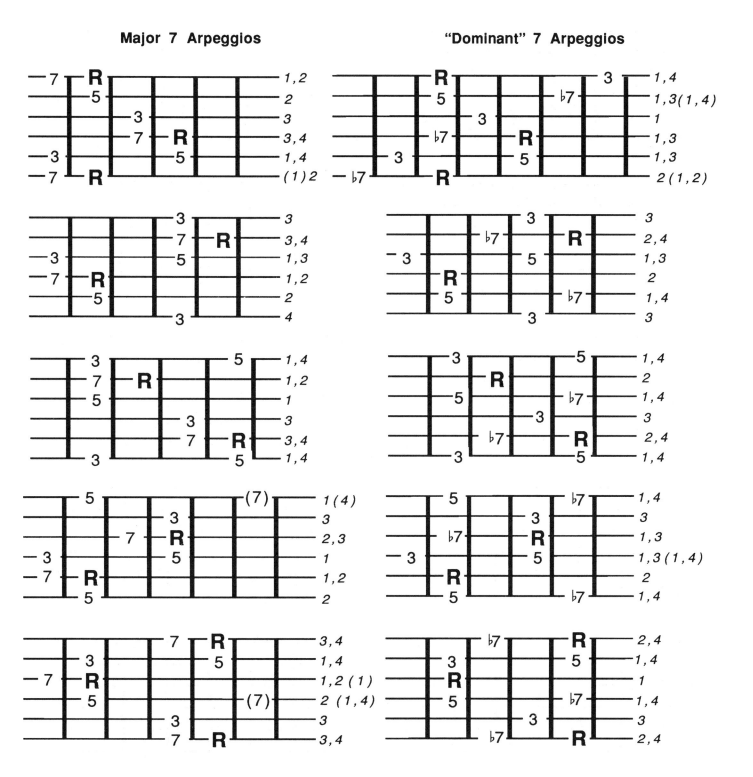

minor/Major 7 Arpeggios

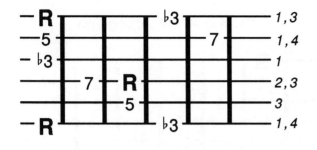

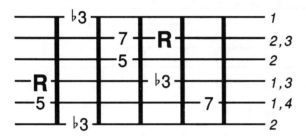

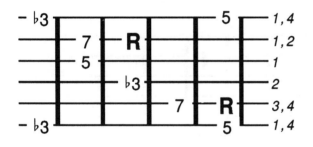

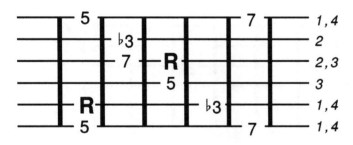

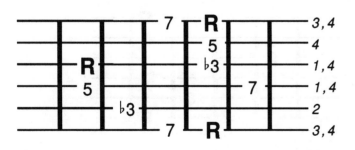

minor 7 Arpeggios

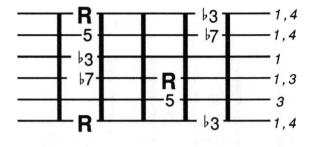

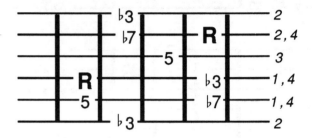

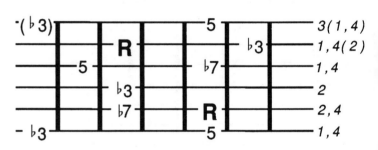

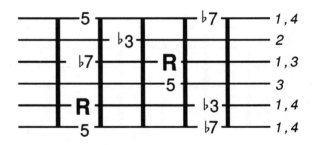

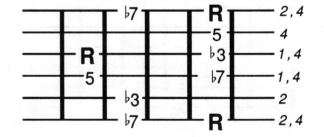

half diminished 7 Arpeggios

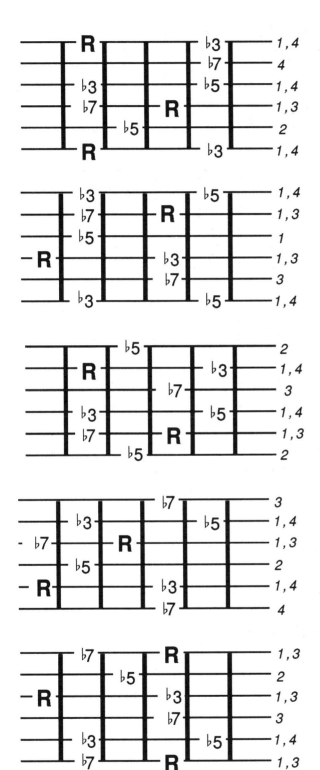

diminshed 7 Arpeggios

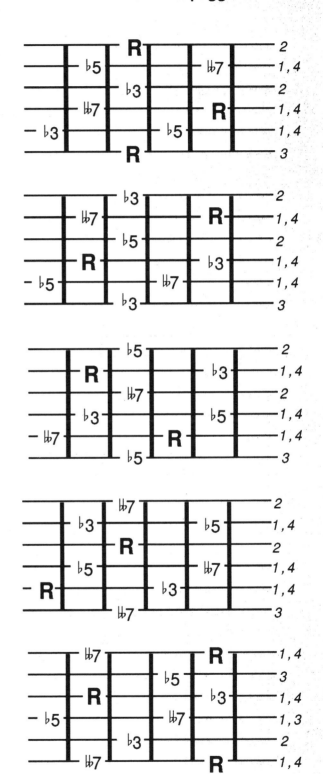

Major 6 Arpeggios

Augmented 7 Arpeggios

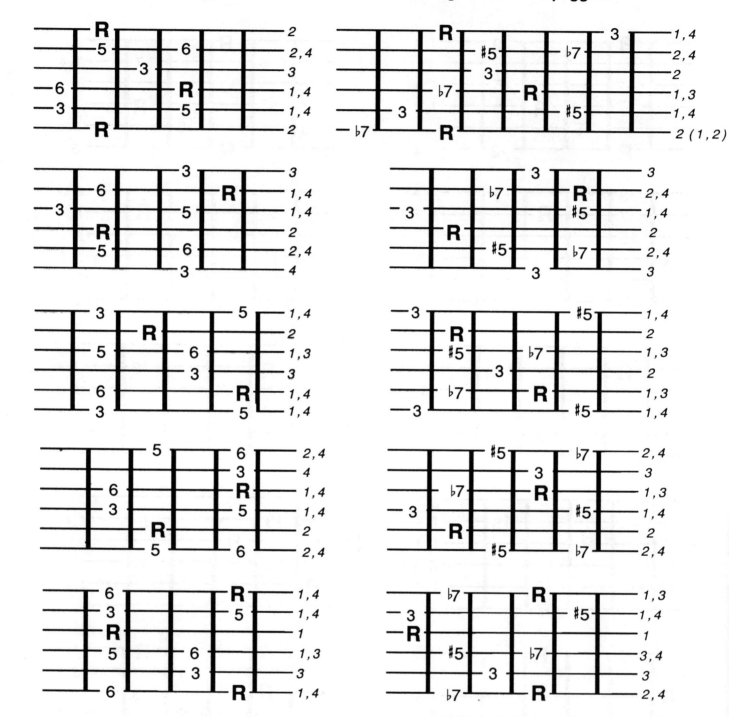

APPENDIX 5: *Some Basic Chord Forms*

Major Chords

Minor Chords

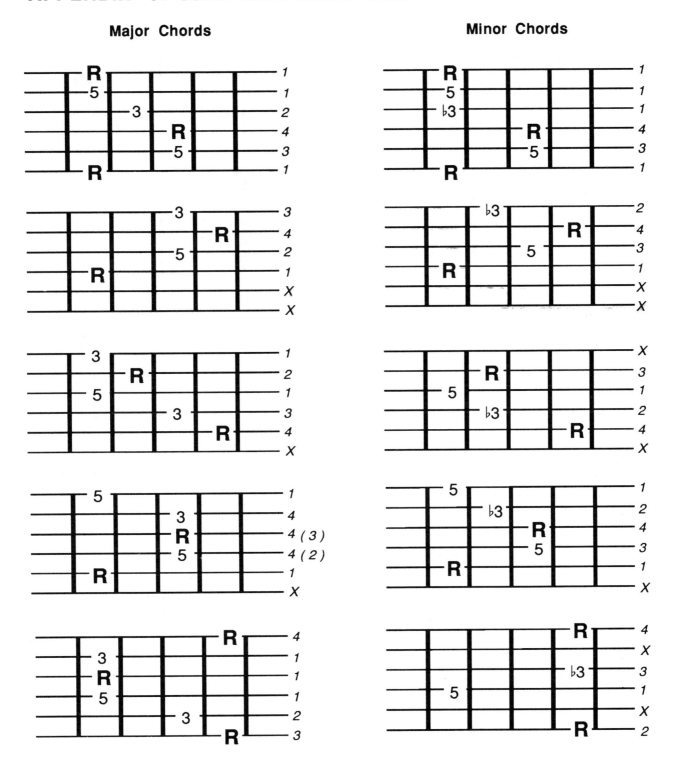

Augmented Chords

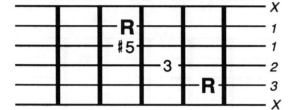

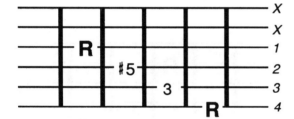

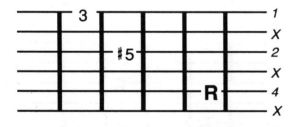

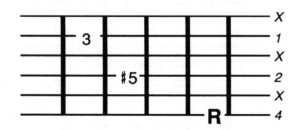

Diminished Chords

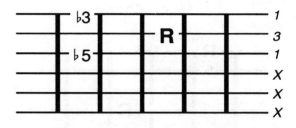

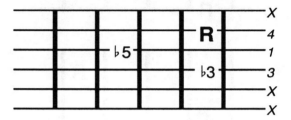

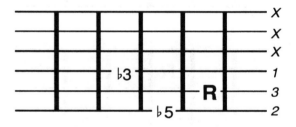

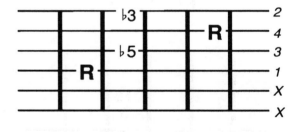

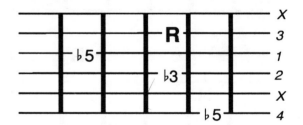

Major 7 Chords

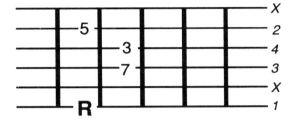

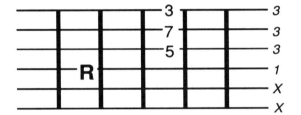

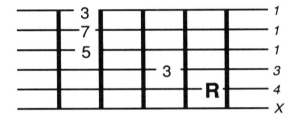

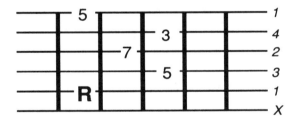

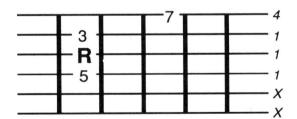

"Dominant" 7 Chords

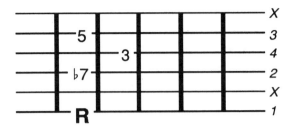

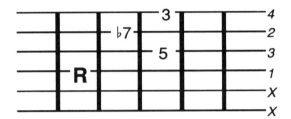

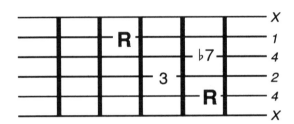

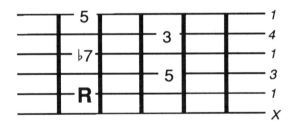

minor/Major 7 Chords

minor 7 Chords

half diminished 7 Chords

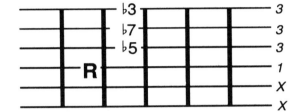

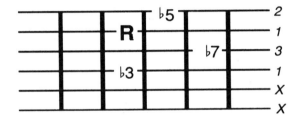

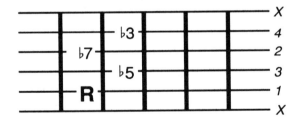

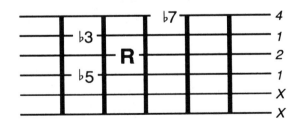

Diminished 7 Chords

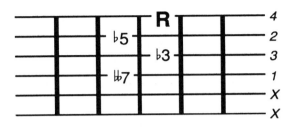

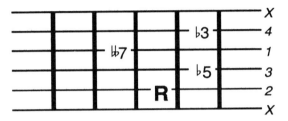

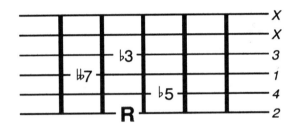

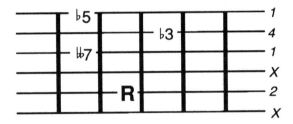

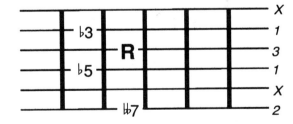

Augmented 7 Chords

Major 6 Chords

APPENDIX 6: Some Chord "Maps"

Major 7 Chord Map

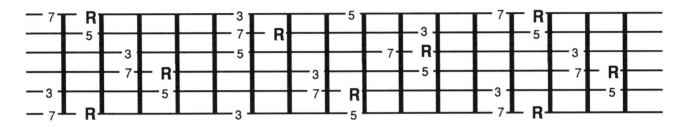

"Dominant" 7 Chord Map

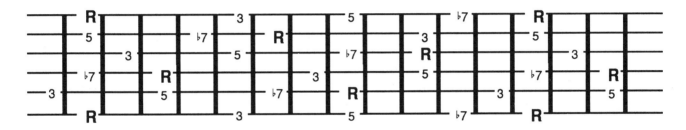

minor 7 Chord Map

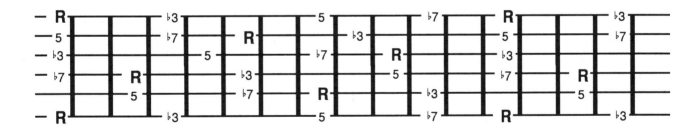

minor/Major 7 Chord Map

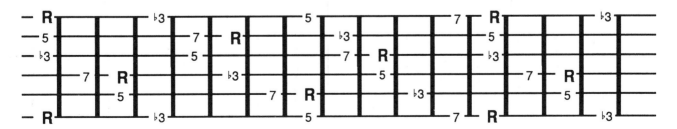

half diminished 7 Chord Map

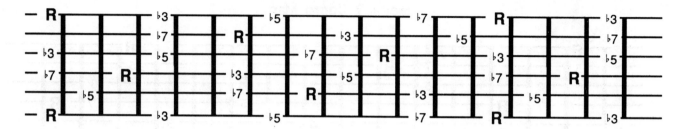

diminished 7 Chord Map

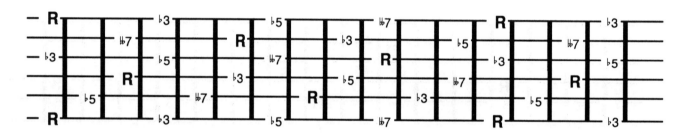

Augmented 7 Chord Map

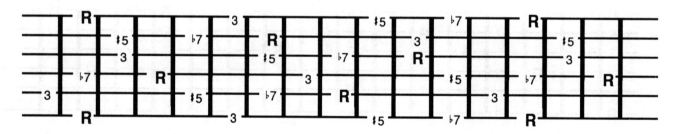

Major 6 Chord Map

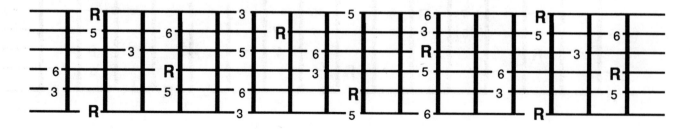

Major 13 Chord Map

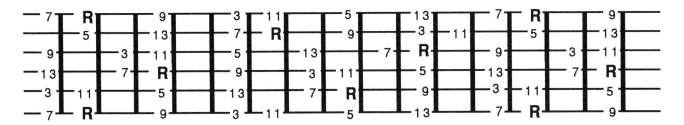

"Dominant" 13 Chord Map

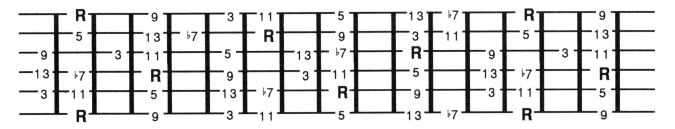

Altered "Dominant" 13 Chord Map

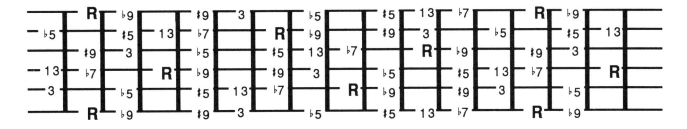

minor 11 Chord Map

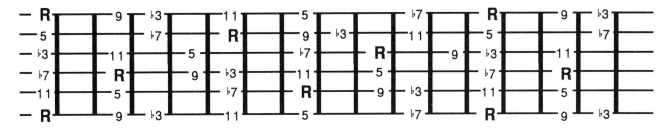

APPENDIX 7: Blank Diagrams

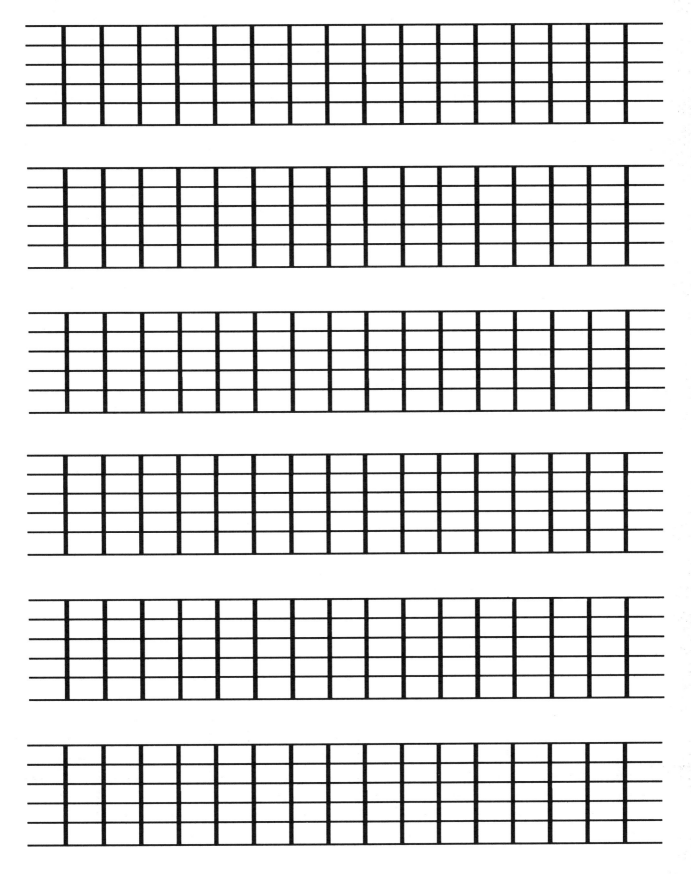

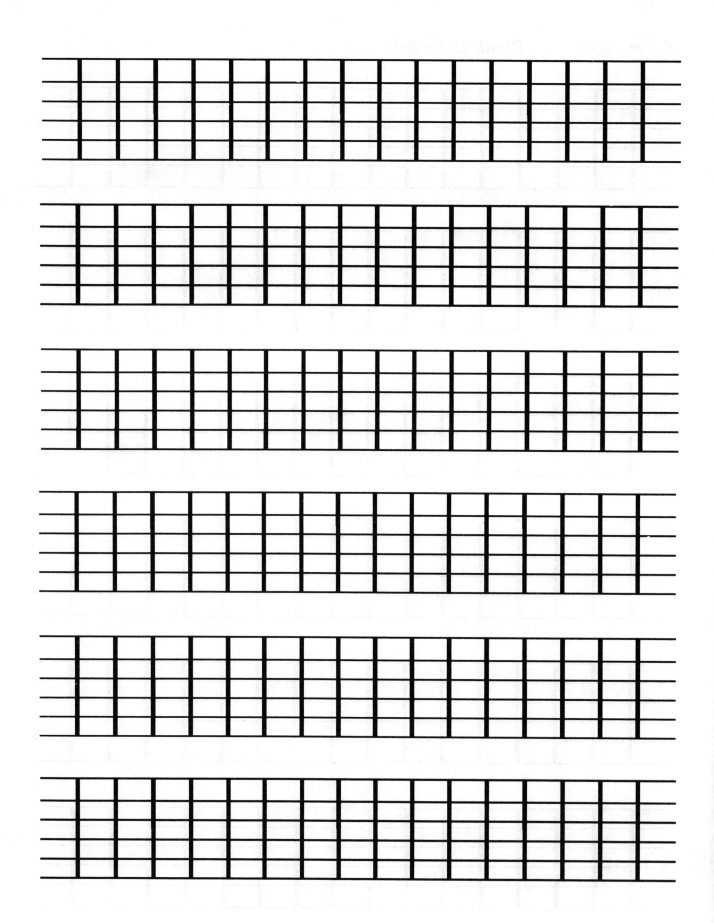

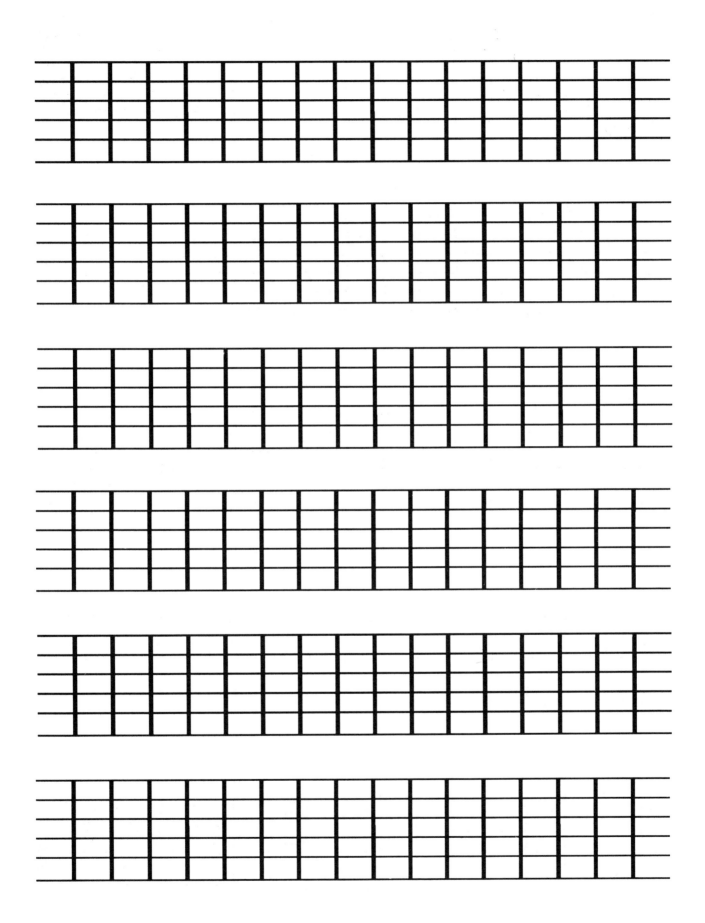

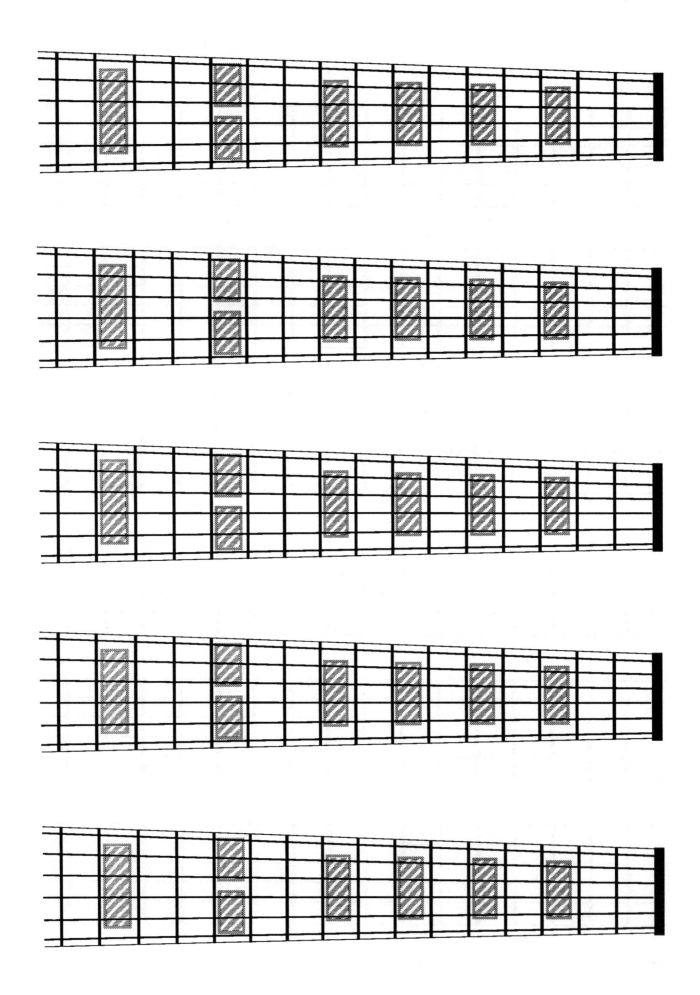

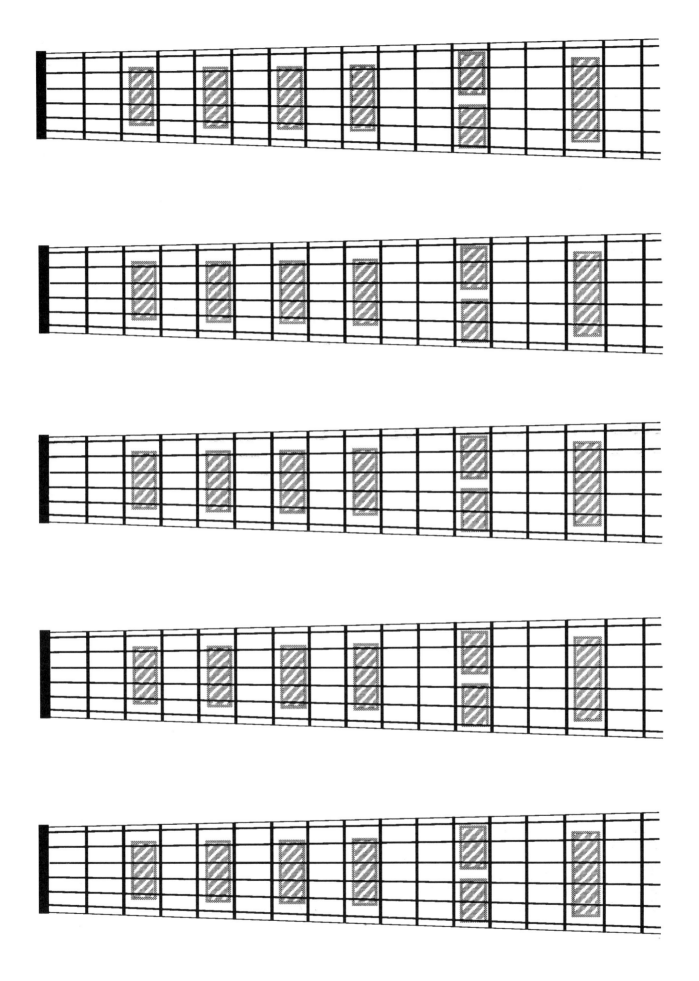

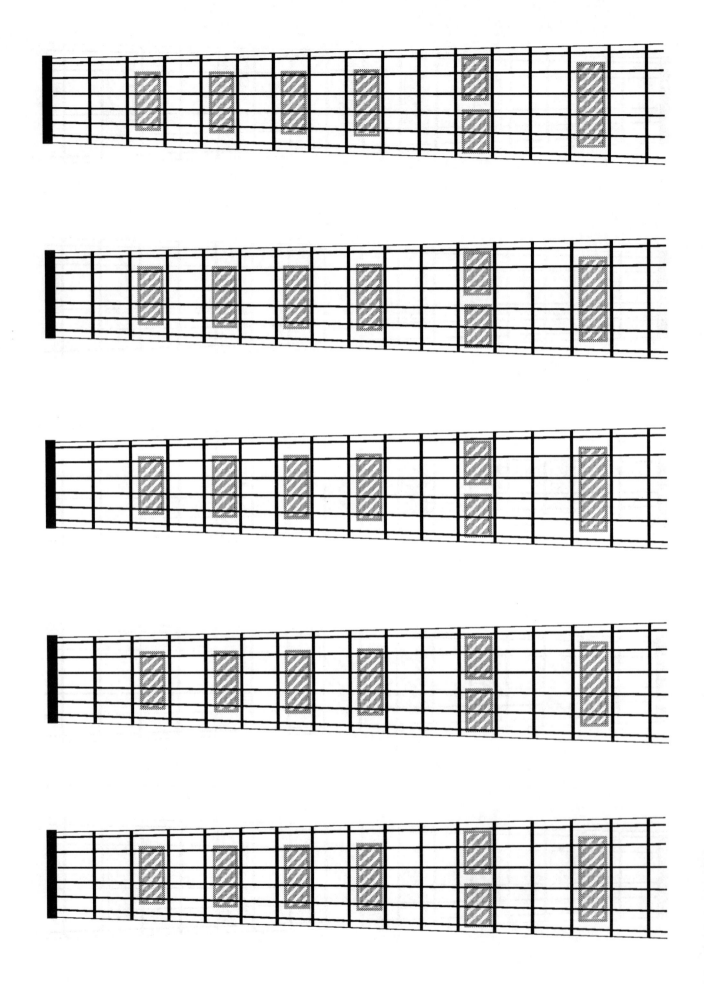

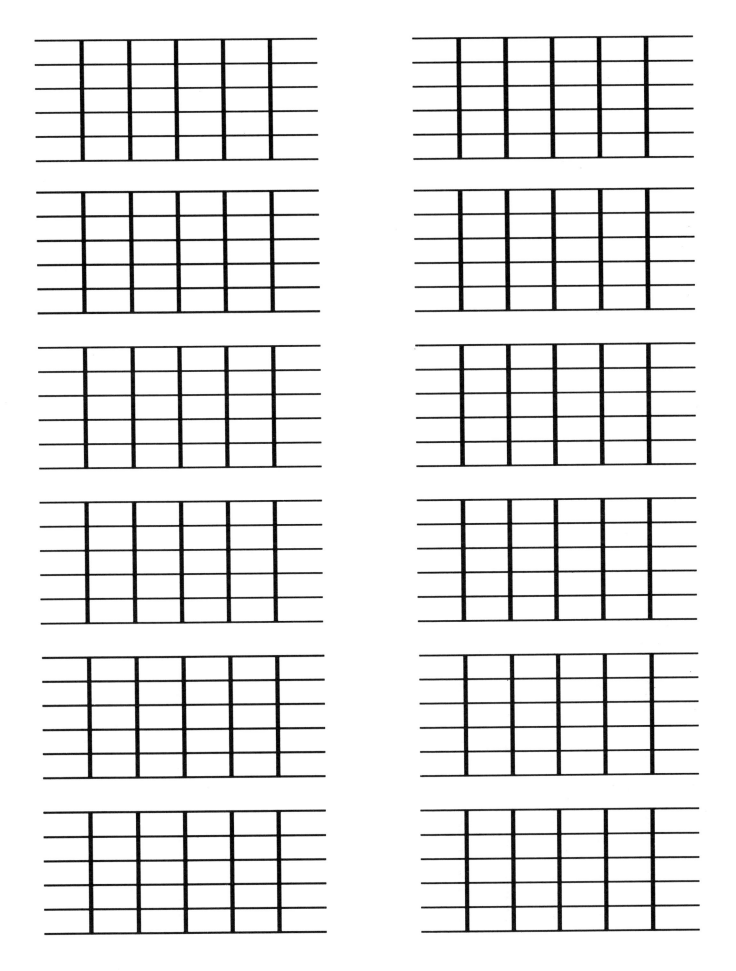

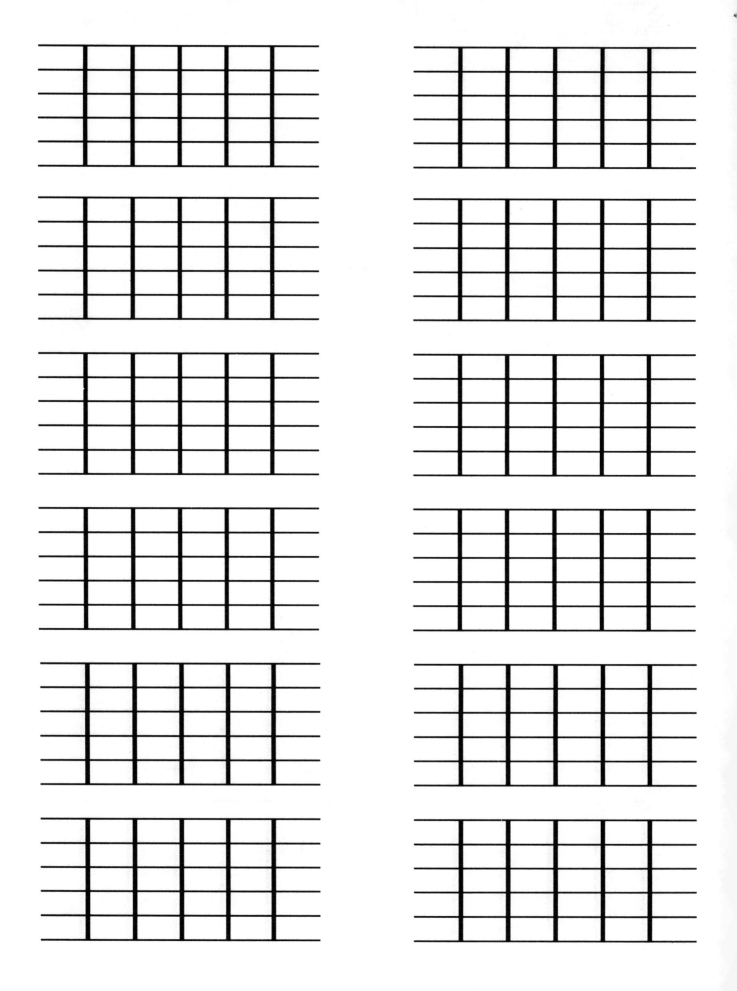

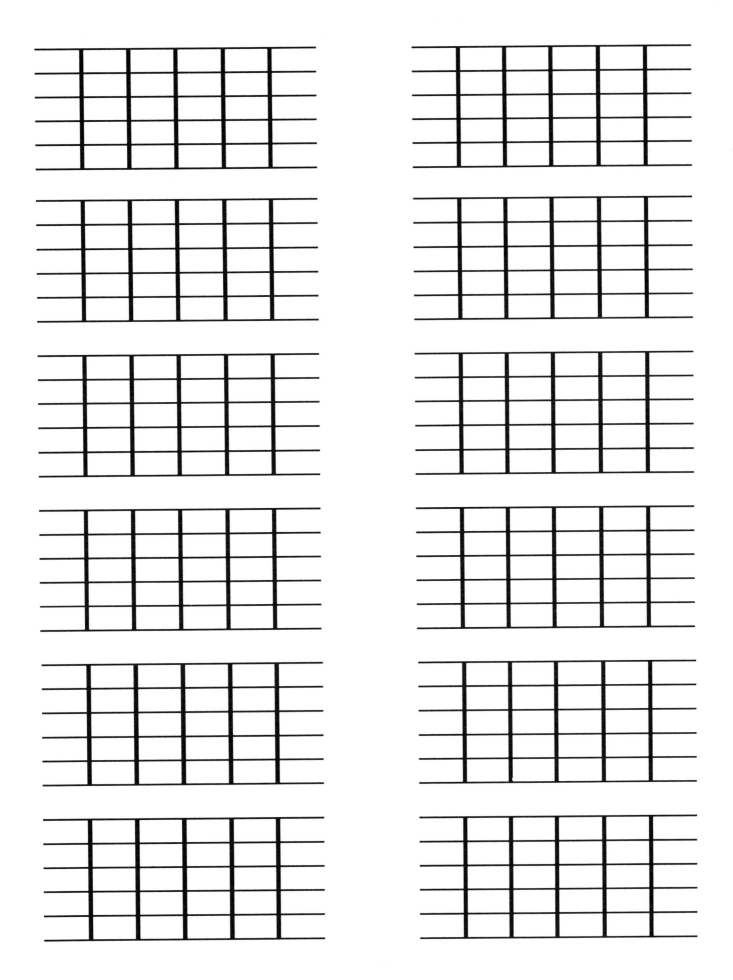

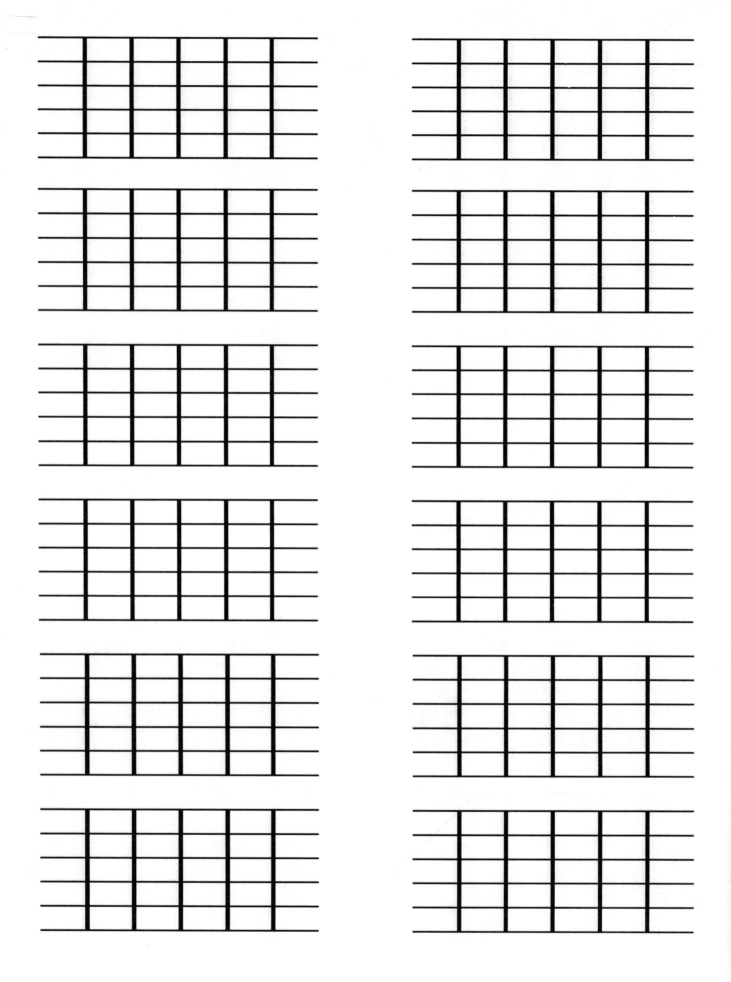

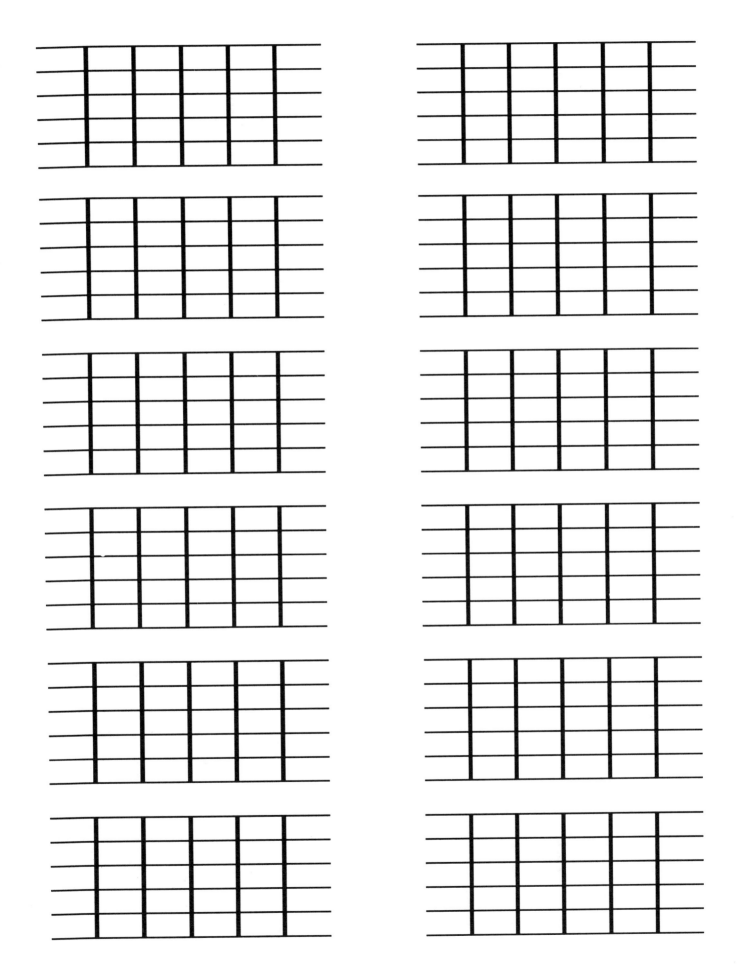

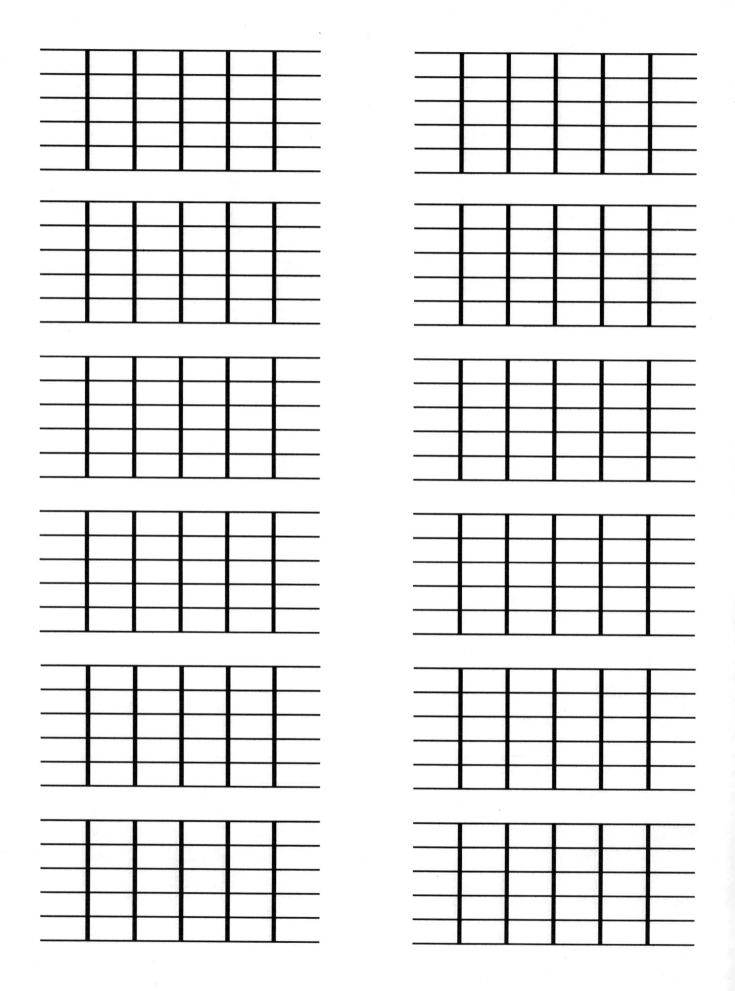